How to Win Customers
With Google Ads

A Practical Jargon Free Guide For

CEOs And Business Owners

How to Win Customers
With Google Ads
A Practical Jargon Free Guide For
CEOs And Business Owners

Written by

Ajay Dhunna

Win Customers With Google Ads
A Practical Jargon Free Guide For CEOs and Business Owners
© 2022 Digital Search Academy Ltd T/A Ajay Dhunna Digital

ISBN: 9798353624271 Paperback

Edited By: Ajay Dhunna

The strategies in this book are presented primarily for enjoyment and educational purposes. Every effort has been made to trace copyright holders and obtain their permission for the use of copyright material.

The information and resources provided in this book are based on the authors' personal experiences. Any outcome, income statements or other results, are based on the authors' experiences, and there is no guarantee that your experience will be the same. There is an inherent risk in any business enterprise or activity, and there is no guarantee that you will have similar results as the author as a result of reading this book.

The author reserves the right to make changes and assumes no responsibility or liability whatsoever on behalf of any purchaser or reader of these materials.

Get Free Lifetime updates of this book.
Visit www.ajaydhunna.com/google-book

Claim Your Free Website & Google Ads Review.
Visit www.ajaydhunna.com/freereview

Remember to. Download your PPC Worksheet which I will refer throughout this book.

Download the worksheet here:

www.AjayDhunna.com/ppcworksheet

"Reading books or video training won't make you an expert, however taking actions and implementations will!"

Index

1) Dedication

I dedicate this book, to my son, Aryan Dhunna, who is the light of my life. He is by far my biggest fan and supporter. Always questioning what I am doing, why, and how, all of which I love, and makes me proud to see him growing up as an inquisitive and bright young lad. He was the one who passingly once told me I should write a book… this was when he co-authored a book which got published when he was around 10 years of age. It seeded in my mind until one day, I knew it had to be done. I knew it was time for me to serve other CEOs, business owners and marketing managers by putting my wealth of knowledge on Google Ads into a book which will help them. Aryan is one of the few people whom I can count on one hand, who has been questioning the progress and nature of my book. Thank you, Aryan, you're my rock, and one in a million!

2) Acknowledgements

Being a techy, I needed guidance and a push to transfer the knowledge inside my head onto paper, to help serve others. There are so many I would like to thank during this journey of writing my first book.

I have already mentioned my son, Aryan Dhunna, who has truly been my backbone. Everything I do, I do it for you son. Thank you for supporting and believing in me.

I also want to give a special thank you to my mentor, James Nicholson. Back in 2020, right at the start of the global pandemic, I was lost, and at my all-time low, especially having lost some loved ones. It was you who helped me to re-focus, to help me believe in myself, supported me in my business during the last couple of years and persuaded me to write this book. I'm eternally grateful to you!

I thank my team for helping and guiding me throughout the process of writing this book as well as inspiring me and forcing sleepless nights upon me.

A massive thank you to Petrina Ten who voluntarily offered to read my book and do the initial proof-reading! You're a legend!

Thank you Jody Raynsford who has always been my *go to pro* for any advice/guidance I needed on copy-writing as well as creating awesome ad copy!

I know I should be listing many others here, but for now, I'd just like to say a massive Thank you to everyone that has been there for me including my friends, family, dad, mum and my wife.

Equally, I'd love to thank all those, who have never supported, discouraged me to write a book, told me to quit business and get a 9-5 job, never believed in me or never been there for me, as without you, this would never have been possible! You know who you are, you fuelled me, and I'll be eternally grateful to you. ☺

3)   Praise

James Nicholson, Business Growth Academy

Having read this awesome book written by Ajay, and having known Ajay for the last 5 years, I can see he has put all his knowledge and expertise on Google Ads into it, as well as his personality and humour. Ajay has a very methodical approach when it comes to implementing Google Ads campaigns. I've also benefited so much from his knowledge of Google Ads, particularly when it comes to building great Google Ads campaign which work very well, optimising Google Ads accounts as well as understanding how keywords really work, and the mistakes to avoid. Ajay has worked extremely hard on this very well-written book. Well done Ajay!

Nari Hakobyan, Google

I've worked with Ajay over the course of 3 years whilst being employed for Google and, throughout that time, he has been totally serving the needs of his clients with scrupulous eye to every detail in the process. From daily strategic talks to high commitment to results, Ajay has been doing his level best to aim for success.

This book is indeed a true reflection of his perfect knowledge of Google Ads, more specifically on what to do to make more money from it rather than the vice versa. I can relate to everything he says in the book. Ajay has a great ability to explain complicated scenarios in a very simple-to-understand way. Ajay has a very structured approach to managing and optimizing Google Ads campaigns as well as how he sets them up in the first place. Ajay's knowledge and skills on Google Ads is tremendous. He knows exactly what it takes to help businesses generate more leads and sales. It's been an absolute pleasure working with Ajay, and he truly deserves a lot of success from his book.

Guy Littlejohn, Founder, Consultancy. Ex, Google

Having worked at Google (UK) for 3 years as a Google Ads Account Manager, I have seen how hard Ajay works to create Google Ads campaigns which are profitable at a very early stage. This book is a true reflection of Ajay's expertise in how he goes about building successful and profitable campaigns. He uses a 7-step system which he has explained very well in this book. Ajay has many years of experience in creating, optimizing and reporting on Google Ads, and it has been such a pleasure to read his book, which is a must-have for any business owner.

Amitab Dev, Business Head at Bruce Clay India

I'm the Business Head at Bruce Clay India, a world-renowned SEO agency. I've known Ajay since my days at RankWatch in 2018, where we were involved in a project to create reporting tools for Google Ads. I have continually watched Ajay go from strength to strength when it comes to Google Ads, and his knowledge on the subject is phenomenal! I have been privileged to have been given the opportunity to read Ajay's book and can honestly say, every CEO, Business Owner and Marketing Manager must read it if you are involved in Google Ads in any shape or form. A very easy-to-read, understandable and logically written book! Great work Ajay Dhunna!

4)   "Google Ads don't work!"?

I get it all the time!! You can bet your bottom dollar I hear this at least once a month from potential customers. So how does the conversation usually go? Here goes (I'm cutting it short of course)…

Customer: Hi, we want to get more traffic via SEO (that's **S**earch **E**ngine **O**ptimization) to get our website listed at the top of Google, but we do not wish to use Google Ads.

Me: Sure, no problem. But before I tell you more about our services, have you considered other options such as Google Ads?

Customer: No, Google Ads doesn't work!

Me: Why not?

Customer: We ran it a while and lost all our money on it, and conversions were poor.

Me: OK. So who created and ran your Google Ads?

Customer: We did.

Me: How much experience do you have of running Google Ads?

Customer: I've just started!

And there you have it. 99% of the time, there lies the answer as to why they **thought** Google Ads doesn't work.

Unsurprisingly, over 60% of potential customers who say this to me, end up becoming my Google Ads customers!

I give it to you straight. It's not that Google Ads doesn't work. It's usually the case that the Google Ads account was not set up properly and managed by someone who didn't understand exactly how it works.

I love cars. I love to drive nice sports cars, feeling every bump of that road, whilst listening to that engine purr whilst I put my foot down on the gas. But would I dare to lift the bonnet of the car, tune the fuel injectors, change the spark plugs, tune the air intake, only because I've read a book on "Dummies Guide To Tuning A Car Engine", and then put the car on the motorway? No chance…

Not unless I have years of experience behind me in tuning car engines, have the right tools, I've undergone some formal training, or I am accompanied by an expert, who 'hand-holds' me as to what nut and bolt to turn, and when.

The same goes with Google Ads: To get great results from Google Ads, you need to understand how it works, what defines a Good or Bad, and which "cogs" you need to turn to help you create a profitable Google Ads account right from day one! Try guess working and it will only result in letting you down. As they say, a good workman never blames his tools. And neither should you, i.e. Let's not blame Google!

Knowledge is power. Following a system is what you need. A proven system which has been tried and tested to work, time and time again.

Google Ads is exactly the same as the example of fixing your sports car which I gave above. If managed poorly, it's going to give you poor results back. I call this GIGO. Garbage-In-Garbage-Out. If you do a garbage job of managing your Google Ads, you are going to get garbage results. When managed well, Google Ads is a gold-mine for any business. It requires skill. An understanding of how each cog of the system works. Just like a car engine. Turn the wrong cogs, and your Google Ads will suffer, whereas knowing which cogs to turn and when, could instantly start delivering you a constant stream of leads and sales.

I'm not implying you have to be the best in the world. You just have to know how Google Ads functions. You need to know what knowledge you have which you can capitalize on, and where you might need that extra hand holding.

Did you know, you can even tell Google Ads what your objectives are? For example, you can tell Google Ads that you wish to set up a campaign to drive you lots of conversions (Leads). Or you can tell Google Ads that you don't mind having less leads, but you want each lead to cost you a certain amount (i.e. £20 per lead, or you are looking for an ROI of 5:1.

It's all there. You just have to have the knowledge to know what you wish to achieve, then knowing how to achieve it, is the easy part.

What is even more scary is how many so-called agencies or freelancers I come across that have managed Google Ads accounts so poorly, it's quite shocking. By nature, I have always encouraged all my customers to take a step back and really have a good think about what they are hoping to achieve first. And then consider if they have the foundations ready to help them achieve that, like their website? Have they got the resources available to manage their campaigns, as well as the number of leads/sales they get, i.e. the infrastructure? I see reports given to clients by agencies, which are not worth the paper they are written on. This is what I am hoping to clarify and educate people who read this book. Knowing what to look out for.

So next time someone says to you, Google Ads doesn't work. Just ask them, who set it up in the first place and what's their experience? Knowledge is power. Whether you are managing Google Ads yourself, your staff is managing it for you, or even your agency/freelancer. If you understand how it works, you are in a much better boat to talk to them at their level and take no cr@p from them. Good knowledge gives you the ammunition to ask the right questions, which then gives you the right answers, allowing "You" to decide, what's not working, what may not be working, as well as giving you the knowledge to suggest next steps.

This is precisely why I wrote this book. Not to make you the next Einstein of Google Ads. But to give you enough knowledge to help steer your business, by understanding the fundamentals of Google Ads, and more importantly, understanding a system you can follow to build success and profitable Google Ads campaigns right from the start.

On a final note, a famous quote from one of the founders of Google…

"Optimism is important. You have to be a little silly about the goals you are going to set. There is a phrase I learned in college called, 'having a healthy disregard for the impossible.' That is a really good phrase. You should try to do things that most people would not do."

- Larry Page

5) My Promise To You

I want you to understand, I'm writing this book myself. It's not a book written by a ghost-writer who has collated information from various sources and put it together. And what that means, is everything in this book is from my own personal experience, from what I have gained over the last 20 years or so. What I say in this book works. And it's taken me years to work out, which I'm giving to you on a plate.

What I do promise is total transparency. I have a No-BS approach to everything both in business as well as personal life. I consider myself very straight talking, so what you will get is my thoughts on everything in an unpolished manner, hash tag, raw format!

This book will therefore empower you with knowledge to talk at a competent level with whomever it is you are talking to about Google Ads. Whether that be your marketing agency, or your internal marketing staff, a freelancer or whether it's your clients or even potential clients. That's because you will learn to cut all through the BS that's out there and get straight to the point.

By learning content from this book, you will learn to reassess what you are doing right, what you may be doing wrong, and more importantly, where are the untapped opportunities for growth. Just imagine what this can do to your business. Just imagine what this can do when you ask your marketing agency, or your marketing consultants, questions they just did not expect you to know about, let alone ask about.

What annoys me is when I hear some of my competitors making great claims with customers, just to win their business. Such as "they have inside secrets, they have direct contact with Google, making false promises and mismanaging expectations". Such strategies are short-lived as most the time they are untrue, and customers soon start seeing through the BS. It's important to win the trust of customers you work with. Likewise, it's important for your suppliers (agencies or consultants) to win your trust. The only way to achieve this is by being totally honest, having full transparency, and managing expectations. I'm a great believer of this and hence I have been able to build a successful agency and taught so many people on how to manage Google Ads and similar digital marketing campaigns.

Whatever I teach in this book, I use it day in-day-out and use this to manage a portfolio of currently around $750,000. So I know it works!

I'll let you in on another secret... "Disclaimer... this is just of course just my own opinion :-)"... What Google says or recommends is not always true. I don't always agree with the typical accepted conventional wisdoms that are out there. It's good to assess everything for yourself. For example, Google rewards you for having a great CTR (Click-Through-Rate). Click-Through-Rate is essentially what percentage of people clicked on your Ad against how many times it was shown on the Google page. The exact formula is:

CTR = (Number of times your Ad was Shown on Google (Impressions)) / No. of times your Ad was Clicked) X 100

Funny isn't it. Each time someone clicks on your Ad, Google makes money. Quite ironic Google loves CTR! I have numerous campaigns where the CTR is incredibly low, yet the ROI is absolutely amazing. However, when I look at the Google Ads reports and metrics, it still keeps telling me to improve my CTR! And that's because I have amazingly optimised campaigns and Ads. Ads which will deter people from clicking on them if the service being provided is not suited to them, whilst attracting clicks from very highly, relevant and qualified audiences. So although the Clicks may be low, the quality of the clicks is exceptionally high!

By reading this book, I want you to have the "WOW" factor, "Wow, I didn't know this or that". I almost want you to feel 'cocky', knowing you are armed with powerful information, tools and techniques, to know what it takes, to run a successful Google Ads campaign.

Now here's the thing, even if you don't plan on becoming the next Larry Page or Sergey Brin (the legends who founded Google), you can bet your bottom dollar that by reading this book, you will be able to have a half-decent conversation with your fellow peers about what really makes Google Ads tick, and understanding a tried and tested, proven system to help grow businesses.

At the age of 45, I decided to start practising martial arts, in particular karate. I set a goal that I am going to aim to be a black-belt in karate by the age of 50. I worked damn hard for it and my sensei, Sensei Om Parkash supporting me throughout this journey. What I learnt was, success does not come overnight. You have to work for it, weeks, months or even years. Whether it is learning a new skill set or trying to achieve something in life. Keep at it, work hard... Determination, Persistency and Resilience. Whether you wish to setup a business, learn marketing, or any other goals in your life, these are the values that will help you in your journey to success. Sounds good? Let's move on. ☺

6)   Is this book for you?

This book is for you if...

"You do not need to be a techy! You just have to have the ambition and determination to learn and to succeed in business, whether it be your own, or the organisation you work for."

If you have picked up this book, it is likely you may be the CEO of a company, a business owner, or Marketing Director. It could also be that you have an authoritative role within marketing and have a vested interest in helping to scale up the growth & revenue of a business.

Perhaps you have tried, or are running Google Ads campaigns yourself, whether you personally or your company, and maybe you have realized that there is so much to understand, and a basic superficial knowledge of Google Ads can do more damage than good, whether to your business, or to your clients.

It could also be you have vaguely heard about Google Ads, and want to better understand what it is, how it works and how you can potentially use it to help grow your business. You do not need to be a Google Ads Expert to get value from this book. Neither do you need to even know what it is. I'm going to talk you through it all, right from the very beginning.

Maybe your business right now is not where you want it to be. Or maybe you are just starting out in business, and are looking to grow your business, by getting more sales, more qualified leads, and more enquiries, which ultimately results in more customers.

If you are reading this book, I know you are hungry for success and want to be a leader within your field.

On the Flipside, you may be fearing your competitors may be stealing your business. Maybe you hate losing tenders, you hate losing customers and you hate losing sales. Possibly you blame your staff, your marketing agency, or your freelance consultant if they have not got the knowledge or experience to get your business to where you want it to be.

If you resonate with any of these, please continue reading, as you are certainly in the right place!

I want you to feel in total control of your Google Ads. I don't want you to feel your business may go down, or out of control due to a lack of knowledge, whilst your competitors are *succeeding each* day.

One of the biggest fears a business owner can experience is when their customer moves to their competitor. I want to almost eradicate the possibility of this, especially if it is due to the marketing results you have not achieved.

My sole purpose in this book is to ensure you understand the power behind Google Ads. It's a complex platform, and there is a lot to learn. I want you to have a solid understanding of a methodology to apply, and a system to use, which enables you to step back and look at the entire Google Ads process from a holistic perspective.

I want you to be certain of achieving success & delivering tangible results to grow your business. So much in control that you know you are armed with the best knowledge possible, and if you cannot do it, then you know someone who can, and you know the right questions to ask as well as results to expect.

I come across a lot of people who are tired of listening to the so-called 'experts' advising them to 'do this', and 'do that', or 'we did this' and 'we did that', but it hasn't worked. It normally ends up being a blame-oriented culture, where it is always someone else fault!

This is why I am keen to share with you my "**7 Step Google Ads Fastrack Blueprint**", to ensure your Google Ads campaign is set up correctly from day 1 and is driving a stream of quality leads and sales within a very short period of time. My intention is to help you understand exactly what Google Ads is, how it works, what's the difference between

Google Ads and SEO, Facebook, and the other numerous platforms out there.

Furthermore, my 7-step system ensures you avoid making mistakes, which many people make when setting up their campaigns, i.e. by deep diving straight into Google Ads. The number one cause of many failed Google Ads campaigns is not having the correct foundations in place prior to building the campaign.

I have worked on a variety of different types of businesses, mostly service-based businesses such as dentists, lawyers, marketing agencies, home improvements, and similar types of businesses. I have also worked on numerous e-commerce projects helping businesses to achieve a return on ad spends (ROAS) in excess of 500%! You're definitely in the right place.

This book is not for you if...

There is no such thing as a shortcut to a successful campaign. There is no such thing as instant gratification. I promise you. If that's what you are looking for, I politely request you close this book and go live your life in Bongo-Bongo land.

Gone are the days when you can launch a digital marketing campaign and it can start driving you tons of qualified traffic for free, or at a cost of next to nothing. It takes time. Time, Patience, and a lot of work to optimise. Above all, it requires a good strategy to be put into place. So if you think you can read this book, or any book or course for that matter, and implement a get-rich scheme overnight, you better pack your bags back to planet mars, as it *ain't gonna* happen!

This book is also not for you if you want to become a complete hands-on whiz kid at Google Ads. If that is you, I would like to invite you to check out my courses or mentoring programmes where I can train you, by visiting www.AjayDhunna.com/training. This book really is to introduce Google Ads as well as introduce you to a system. A methodology, which firstly helps you to understand exactly how Google Ads work, and also ensures your Google Ads campaigns have been setup for success, from day one!

This book is certainly not for you if you have no interest in knowing what your marketing team does, in ensuring that your marketing budget is well spent, or if you still believe Google Ads doesn't work and aren't open to being shown why and how they can work.

7)   So why should you listen to me?

My name's Ajay Dhunna, and I'm a digital marketing specialist. I've been implementing digital marketing strategies for the best part of 20 years now, so there is not a lot you can tell me about that I may never have heard of. That being said, I'm always open to learning more, as technology is an ever-evolving cycle of new developments, new platforms, and new strategies.

Having started my first career 20+ years ago, I started as a Software Engineer, developing intranet applications for multi-national companies such as Barclays Bank, KPMG, Npower (Called Midlands Electricity Board back then) to name a few.

I developed a natural interest in marketing, purely by chance. I was intrigued as to how websites are built and how they get traffic. I soon started implementing digital marketing strategies, the first of which was SEO (Search Engine Optimisation). Back in the day, Google was unheard of. It didn't even exist. I remember the first search engine I optimized a website for Excite, Hotbot, Yahoo & Altavista.

Yahoo

Yahoo very quickly became my favourite search engine. Simply because it became one of the most popular search engines. It was undefeatable. The King of all Kings when it comes to search engines. No one could come anywhere near it in terms of the amount of people using it, its popularity and so much more. Very quickly I learned how to get websites listed in Yahoo, which in all fairness was not a lot, but just a little bit of keyword optimisation. I grew my company fast as it was a skill I had that most people did not have, and the number of websites being created was growing steadily.

This continued for years. Same again with Excite, Altavista and of course, Hotbot!

Out of nowhere, almost overnight, came the big G! Google. With simply 1 input bar on its screen, it totally revolutionized the search engine history. It was focused on giving users high quality and highly relevant results according to what users had searched for. It was all about providing the best user-experience possible. Google was simple to use. It was simple to look at; It had no Ads, no News sections on the page, and allowed people to have pure focus, on whatever they were looking for. The other engines since soon went on a rapid exponential decline. Though some still exist, Google has continued to Rule the No. 1 spot where people go to conduct a search for over 2 decades and has since built multiple platforms enabling advertisers to choose how they wish to advertise on Google!

I soon found myself torn between developing web applications and marketing. I had developed some highly sophisticated applications for the likes of KPMG, and Barclays bank as a senior software engineer. I had done everything from database design, designing what screens should look like to provide best user-experience, technical implementations using various coding languages. At the same time, I had figured out how to optimise websites, how to get websites listed at the top of search engines, how to get more traffic onto websites and so much more.

But I had to make a decision as to which route I wanted to take. It was like hitting a crossroad. Technologies for web development were grown rapidly, as were the algorithms used by search engines. Both of which needed proper attention. After a long debate with me and myself, I chose the digital marketing route. I knew it was the right decision as soon as I made it. The rest is all history, and I never looked back since.

Since, I have also trained hundreds of students on various forms of digital marketing throughout my life. I soon developed an ability to talk to customers in a non-technical, jargon free method, with a great commercial understanding of business needs. To better understand what they are looking for and to be able to advise them on what they NEED as opposed to what they WANT.

I have seen a lot of Google Ads campaigns fail miserably. And I have equally seen many go from strength to strength. Finding out why some campaigns work so brilliantly and why many fail has always intrigued me. I have always put a lot of time and money into understanding why this happens.

Through my years of experience, I started to understand that implementing a marketing campaign should not start off with a platform such as Google Ads, Bing Ads (Now Microsoft Ads) or whatever it may be, but the starting point must be to step-back and really analyse what you are trying to achieve, who is your competition, what are your KPIs and so much more.

This then helps to build a solid foundation which can then lead to implementing strategies on a platform of your choice such as Google Ads.

I started putting my experience into a framework, which I can then use again and again. Very soon I realized that Google Ads campaigns that are implemented using this strategy, get far quicker and more positive results. I formed this into a system. I developed a 7-step system, which starts from the absolute basics to the implementation of your Google Ads accounts, as well as reporting and optimization.

As a Google Ads specialist, I have often gone from company to company to either train their staff on Google Ads or to consult with them to help them implement Google Ads strategies. Over the years I am astonished at how many CEOs and Directors of companies don't quite understand what Google Ads really is or how it works or why we need it. Instead, many have referred to it as SEO, which is far from the truth.

Google Ads is typically managed by digital marketing agencies where work gets outsourced to, or internal staff, who somehow, "do something" with Google Ads to help generate leads and sales.

This is where I knew there was a gap in the market, to come up with a book. It reminded me of when my son, Aryan, casually once said, "Dad, you should write a book" (As he co-authored a book at the age of 6 as part of a school project, which then got published). His casual comment hit a chord. Although I did not do it at the time. It was only when I realised the lack of knowledge many CEOs and business owners have about how Google works, I recalled what Aryan had said, and it was like that lightbulb moment.

I need to put my knowledge into a book to help and serve others. I decided to start the journey of writing this book, using my year of experience to help educate CEOs, Business Owners and Directors, about exactly what Google Ads is, how it works, as well as what defines a good structure, what type of methodology to use when implementing Google Ads and so much more.

By understanding this, the readers of this book are then far better equipped to talk to agencies (or staff) at their level. Better understand the terminology they use. Not only that, but this book better helps to arm CEOs and business owners with powerful knowledge of what are the right questions to ask, what types of reports should we get as opposed to the reports we do get, and how Google Ads should be set up right in the first place, how research is conducted and so much more.

I use a data-driven approach. In other words, I base my decisions based on data. Hence why it's imperative to have good quality data. Again, I'm a firm believer of GIGO. For those of you who have attended any of my training courses, would have heard me mention this a million times. GIGO stands for Garbage In Garbage Out. In other words, if you feed a system with Garbage Information, i.e. (**Garbage IN)**, you will end up making Garbage decisions so your outcome will be Garbage too (**Garbage OUT**).

8) Google Ads – Past, Present & Future

Google Ads is a pay-per-click advertising model that underpins the world's most successful search engine.

BTW, if you wish to get straight into the learnings of Google Ads, feel free to skip this section. I wrote this as I felt it was important to get a background on Google and how it came about.

Google was by no means the first search engine on the block. Before it, there was Archie, VLib, Veronica, Jughead, Wanderer, Infoseek, Yahoo, WebCrawler, Lycos, Excite, Alta Vista, and more. **However, what later became Google was initially called BackRub**, though unlike the others, it used a novel way of ranking websites.

Backrub!

Here is the story of how Google grew from an idea cooked up by a couple of university students to a business with around 99,000 employees, and annual revenues of about $140 billion.

Google receives most of that revenue, about $120 billion, from advertising. We will look in some detail at how Google has developed its advertising model, how it works today, and how Google has integrated advertising with organic search.

In the beginning

In 1995, two Stanford University students, Larry Page and Sergey Brin, along with several additional collaborators, created an innovative search engine. They based it on estimating the importance of a web page from the number of times other web pages linked to them, along with the significance of the sites from where the backlinks originated. They called their algorithm PageRank and the search engine BackRub, which a little later became known as Google.

After a year of running Google on university servers, they launched Google.com. Their first investor, Andy Bechtolsheim, wrote them a cheque for $100,000 in 1998, Several other angel investors joined in including Amazon's Jeff Bezos. All together they raised around $1 million.

This was enough money to allow Page and Bib to launch the company working from a friend's garage in Menlo Park, California.

Moving on

By 1999 with a staff of eight they moved to a new home at 165 University Avenue, Palo Alto. They also added a dog called Yoshka to their team and hired their first chef. Later that year they received $25 million in funding from two venture capitalists, an investment that lit the touchpaper.

The start of advertising

Initially, Page and Brin were opposed to funding their project through advertising but eventually came around to the idea. They sold text-based ads associated with the keywords uses entered in their search queries. Eric Schmidt, appointed as Google's Chairman and CEO, played a crucial role in growing advertising revenues.

Here you can see what the Google page first looked like when it was launched in 1998:

Going public

In 2003, Google relocated to an office complex in Mountain View, California, which they subsequently called Googleplex. The following year, in August 2004, Google launched its IPO, offering 19,605,052 shares. The offer price was $85; today, the share price is around $1,600.

Early acquisitions

In 2006, Google acquired YouTube for $1.65 billion, and the following year acquired the internet advertising company DoubleClick for $3.1 billion. Business boomed as businesses that previously advertised on traditional media such as TV and newspapers switched to internet advertising, To accommodate the massive increase in site visits, which reached 3 billion a day in 2011, Google built a global network of data centres. That same year Google acquired the mobile phone company Motorola Mobility, for $12.5 billion. After stripping the company of most of its patents, Google sold it on to Lenovo for $2.91 billion. The patents were needed to protect the IPR of the Android operating system.

Business continued to boom. By 2012 revenues were exceeding $50 billion, and in 2013, Google acquired **Waze**, a GPS app that complimented Google Maps, for $966 million. The following year Google acquired the UK-based AI start-up **DeepMind** for an undisclosed sum estimated to be around $400 million.

Alphabet

In 2015, Google reorganised its corporate structure and created Alphabet Inc with Google handling all the conglomerate's internet-related activities.

Advertising on Google

As we have indicated, Google derives most of its revenue from advertising. Since Google started advertising 20 years or so ago, the advertising model has evolved considerably. In the early days, ads were typically glossy and were clearly advertisements, but today they are barely distinguishable from the organic search results. Sometimes you need to look quite hard to tell organic search results and ads apart. We look at the anatomy of a search engine results page (SERP) below, but first, we will look at the history of advertising on Google and how it has evolved to become the enormous revenue-generating beast it is today.

The first Google ad

The first Google ad appeared on a webpage in January 2000. Back then, Google called the service Premium Sponsorship, and sold text ads directly on a cost per thousand (CPM) basis. It wasn't a commercial success and generated only a little money, though there was potential. Google relaunched the service as AdWords in October 2000 as a pay-per-impression system. This was more successful than before, generating a revenue of $85 million in the first year.

However, there was considerable competition. At the time, another company, Overture (previously Go To) was also selling ads on a pay-per-placement auction self-service basis. Go To was the original developer. Their platform gave advertisers the option of bidding on their ads to appear at the top of SERPs. The Go-To service was highly successful, generating a revenue of $288 million. (Yahoo subsequently acquired the company).

Google introduces AdWords pay-per-click

In 2002, Google relaunched AdWords this time using a pay-per-click (PPC) auction model, similar to but more sophisticated than Overture. With Overture, the more advertisers paid, the higher their ad appeared, making it possible to buy the top placement. The downside was that if only a few people clicked on the ad, it would generate very little money.

Aware of this, Google included "Click-Through Rate" (CTR) into its algorithm as a measure of the relevance of the ad. More relevant ads would receive a higher placement. Thus, even if the competition beat the advertisers' top bid, if site visitors clicked on it more often, then it would still rise in the rankings. The algorithm had a massive impact on the success of AdWords both for Google and for its advertisers.

Google AdSense

Google launched AdSense in 2003 after acquiring Applied Semantics. In this model, web developers can add small JavaScript programs to their web pages that display ads available through the Google network. These may be banner ads or smaller display ads. The intention is to show only ads that are relevant to the web page. The website receives payment when the visitors click the ads. Advertisers pay

Google on either a per-click basis or a CPM model based on the number of impressions.

AdWords rebranded as Google Ads

In 2017, Google rebranded AdWords as Google Ads, though it was more than a simple rebranding. Effectively, Google Ads integrates AdWords and AdSense. The revised format makes it much easier for businesses to advertise on platforms other than Google's SERPs such as YouTube, Google Maps, relevant websites, and across the Google display network.

Everything is in one place, so it can all be managed on a single platform, which is a boon for smaller businesses.

Google launches Smart Campaigns

The following year, Google made it very much more straightforward for advertisers by launching Smart Campaigns, an upgrade of the old Google AdWords Express. Essentially, Smart Campaigns provide a management tool which automates many of the functions of running Google Ads.

Advertisers set their marketing goals, geographical targeting, and the products and services they wish to market. The platform will suggest options based on the business type, and once advertisers select them, help create ads and optimise advertising budgets. After launching the campaign, it is easy to monitor the performance of keywords and phrases, adjusting where necessary.

Google shopping

Google launched Google Shopping in 2012 as part of the AdWords package and is now integrated into Google Ads. The model allows advertisers to share data from their online store with Google. Google uses the data to produce product boxes that display an image and other data such as price and sellers' name. Google Shopping has proven to be a highly effective advertising strategy. We give an example below.

Customers can also go to the Google Shopping homepage and search directly from there for specific items. Google shopping has had a significant impact on the way retailers market their products. As a response to the COVID-12 pandemic, Google has made Google Shopping a free service to assist retailers in rebuilding their businesses following the downturn.

The anatomy of Google search engine results page (SERP)

The face of Google advertising has changed considerably. In the early years of AdWords, ads appeared above and to the right of organic search results. The ads were clearly distinguishable.

Over the next few years, Google regularly tinkered with the ads, changing their colour schemes and positioning. They carried out countless experiments to discover what works best. We all know what a modern SERP looks like, we see them every day, but from an SEO viewpoint, it is worth analysing them in more detail.

The first thing to note is that the page's appearance varies considerably depending on what you are searching. For instance, if you are searching for a product such as "rugby balls" the page might look something like this. The advertisements are clearly visible at the top of the page, and the organic search results are immediately below. The adverts in this screenshot are an example of ads generated by Google Shopping, which, as we say above, was launched in 2012.

However, if you are searching for information, for instance, "investment banking", the page is likely to be very different. Here you will see ads at the top of the page underneath a small "Ad" logo, the organic search results below that, and in this case an information box on the right.

If you then scroll down the page, you will see three more ads below the organic search results. The total number of ads on the first page of this search was 7, and there were ten organic search results.

Searches related to investment banking

investment banking uk	investment banking internship
investment banking services	investment banking industry
investment banking salary	investment banking degree
investment banking jobs	investment banking courses

Gooooooooooogle ›

1 2 3 4 5 6 7 8 9 10   Next

9) How does Google Ads work?

The Digital Marketing Success Triad™

I wanted to include this section as I'm truly passionate about it. I tell all my potential customers about it at the start of each project. And that's to help manage expectations. It helps customers get away from the popular misconceived belief that "all they need to do" is to hire a Google Ads specialist, or setup a Google Ads account, and it will become a licence to print money. Far from it, I'm afraid.

The success of a digital marketing campaign is largely dependent on 3 core pillars, which I call, "**The Digital Marketing Success Triad**™"

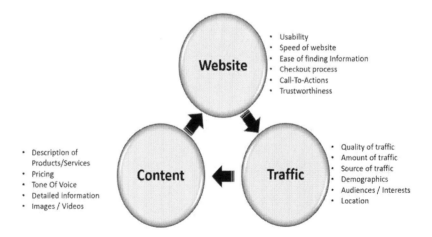

- Usability
- Speed of website
- Ease of finding Information
- Checkout process
- Call-To-Actions
- Trustworthiness

- Description of Products/Services
- Pricing
- Tone Of Voice
- Detailed information
- Images / Videos

- Quality of traffic
- Amount of traffic
- Source of traffic
- Demographics
- Audiences / Interests
- Location

These are:
1) Website
2) Traffic
3) Content

Let me explain this…

Website: Some of the main factors which influence the success of your website are things like usability, speed of website etc (As described per image below). Now let's say you had the best website, however, let's say the **traffic** to your website was poor (maybe low quality or irrelevant, or even not enough traffic), or the **content** on your website was poor (i.e. poor images, products or services not properly described, then your entire marketing campaign will fail.

Traffic – Similarly, let's say you had the best marketing campaign. In other words, you got traffic for all the best keywords for your business and you were getting lots of clicks to your website. However, if your **website** sucked, or you're the **content** on your website was poor, the whole marketing campaign will fail.

Content – Last but not least, let's say you had the best quality content, but your **website** was poorly designed or the quality of your **traffic** was poor, the whole marketing campaign will fail.

Why am I telling you this and what is the significance of the "Digital Marketing Success Triad"? What I'm getting at, is you need to be working as a team. Your web developers, your marketing team, your content writers, all need to be working as a close-knit team so that when sales or leads are low, it doesn't become a blame culture, but you work out collectively, which area of the Digital Marketing Success Triad you need to resolve. Which part or even parts of the triad could be causing the low number of expected leads or sales?

To help implement the Digital Marketing Success Triad, I came up with a system. A system which takes you from the ground up on creating a Google Ads campaign, with fast success of the campaign being in the forefront. I call this system "**7 Step Google Ads Fastrack Blueprint**"

Essentially Google Ads works on an auction system. There are 3 main components when it comes to Google Ads:
1) The customer – This is the person who does the search on Google for a particular keyword.
2) The Advertiser – The advertiser is the person who will pay Google each time someone who has searched for one of their keywords, will click on the Ad.
3) Google – Google will then process the keywords which a user has typed in and depending on which advertiser is bidding for those keywords, Google will use an auction system to determine which advert gets shown on the Google page, and more importantly, at what position on Google.

The "Ad Rank" is ultimately what determines what position Google decides to display Ads on, which is based on your Bid price (i.e. how much you are willing to pay per click) and Quality Score.

Quality Score

Your Quality Score is the most important element that will determine the amount you need to bid on keywords to determine which position your ads get displayed on the search engine results pages. The higher your Google Quality Score, the less you will have to pay for your ad to appear on the Google page.

Quality score is determined by 3 main factors:

- **Ad Relevance** - how relevant is your Advertisement which a user sees, in relation to what they may have searched for.
- **Expected Click-Through-Rate** – This is Google's estimation of the rate at which your potential viewers will actually click on your ad to visit your website or landing page.
- **Landing Page Experience** – This refers to the quality of the experience that a customer has whilst they visit your website or landing page.

Quality score is then reported as a score from 1 to 10.

Bid

The bid is the maximum amount an advertiser will pay to list their advertisement onto the Google page, for a given keyword. However, depending on your Quality Score,

Google will decide how much you are charged. The higher your quality score the less you need to pay.

Ad Rank

As discussed earlier, Ad rank is simply a number which determines which position your Advertisement gets displayed at:

AD Rank = Maximum Bid X Quality Score

Anatomy of a Google Ads account

Let's understand how a Google account looks like, in other words, its anatomy. A Google Ads account should ideally only be built for 1 business. if you have several businesses, I advise you to create separate Google Ads accounts for each of the businesses. In this way, all the reporting, main settings, goals, are all kept focused to that business only, as well as ease of management.

The anatomy of a Google Ads account seems pretty straightforward.

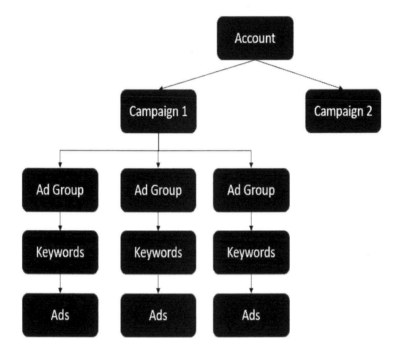

We will discuss all parts of a Google Ads account later, but as a summary, we have:

1) **Account** – As discussed earlier this would ideally belong to just one business, with its own time zones, payment currencies, billing details.

2) **Campaign**: Each account can have many campaigns. Think of campaigns as filing drawers. In a filing drawer, you would keep all your paperwork in separate drawers. Like your bills, insurances, personal paperwork etc. So Campaigns work in a similar way, you can separate your overall products or services separated and organised. In this way, they can all be managed separately, each with its own

ways of how they are set up. In actual face, each Google Ads account can have up to 10,000 campaigns. I have yet to come across an account that even has 10% of that!

3) **Ad Groups**. Again, using the example of a filing cabinet, within each drawer you can have dividers to subdivide your paperwork. For Bills you might have electricity bills, eating bills and so on. In the same way, Ad groups allow you to subdivide your campaigns so that each one of more specific. Interesting fact, you can have up to 20,000 Ad groups. I usually advise having in the region of 5 to 10 Ad groups per campaign.

4) **Keywords**. Each Ad group has keywords. Keywords are what you want your Ads to show on the Google page, which relates to your products or services. I always advise no more than around 20 keywords per Ad group.

5) **Ads**. These are the text-based Ads that your users will see on the Google page when they search for your products or services. We will again discuss these in more detail later.

Google today and in the future

Google is extraordinarily successful. It now has over 90% of the worldwide search engine market, it carries out 63,000 searches per second, and its current market value is around $739 billion. While we have mentioned some of Google's significant acquisitions, it owns many more, approximately 200 other companies.

But what of the future? Google has never stood still; the business has always had an eye on the future. Of course, there is the possibility that Google has become so big that governments might force it to break up into smaller entities, though it's difficult to see how this might be achieved. Even if it does happen, the Google Ads and organic search models are inseparable and will still grow and improve. However, the whole of the search landscape could change as Artificial Intelligence (AI), machine learning and associated technologies increase their impact.

The future of Google Ads

AI and machine learning will impact Google Ads significantly. This is where such technologies will do most of the heavy lifting for you in terms of targeting your potential customers, knowing who to target more aggressively based on the likelihood of them converting into a sale or lead, and vice versa. These so-called "Smart Campaigns" will utilise such technologies to help create more efficient campaigns. We have described these above, and while they make the life of an advertiser much easier, they are still far from perfect. One weakness is that they still use widely fashioned keywords. In any campaign choosing the right keywords is critical. Get them wrong, and your campaign will fail to deliver and go over budget. Choosing the right keywords is a skill within itself.

In future, Google Ads will use AI and machine learning more effectively. For instance, as the amount of available data on advertising campaigns increases, AI will become far better at selecting and fine-tuning the most effective keywords for your campaign. Rather than defining keywords, you would need to merely set your goals and let AI take over from there. AI could also monitor your campaign in real-time, making fine adjustments to your ads and intelligently targeting your prospects. I'm reluctant to say the quality of the recommendations Google's AI makes today, is perfect, far from it to be honest. I look at these daily. Whenever Google says, "I recommend these keywords", on a good day I would use less than 20% of its recommendations.

But of course, there are dangers. Many advertisers are wary that AI is effectively a black box and that there is the potential to lose control of our campaigns. Do we want to hand our advertising over to a machine? If we lose the transparency of our campaigns, how can we manage them should things go wrong? AI has the potential to make Google Ads better, but we do need to handle it with care.

10) Intro to my 7 Step Google Ads Fastrack Blueprint

It's fair enough to say you want to set up a Google Ads campaign. I've heard it all before.

"Setup a Google campaign and it starts giving you a flood of leads and sales straight away"… This is so far from the truth and is just utter BS!

But there is little point in starting off a Google Ads campaign without really understanding what you hope to achieve from it, how much budget you have and so much more.

It's one of the all-time classic mistakes over 50% of businesses make, deep diving into Google Ads without the preparation. Here's a question for you…. *"Would you build a house of bricks if you did not have the architectural drawings ready, the foundation built strong, knowing where you want the doors and windows to be?"* I don't think so, as if you do, your house will probably crumble before it's even built.

Your Google Ads campaign is just the same.
You need a framework to work from. A system. One that has been tried and tested. And more importantly where unlike a lot of courses and systems I have seen, step 1 or 2 is certainly NOT "Creating the Google Ads Campaign", but to create a solid foundation first.

As mentioned earlier, in my early days after graduating from university, I was a software engineer. It was only here that I learnt the importance of preparing to code before coding. Without preparation, you're working on a ticking time bomb.

"Failing To Prepare Is Preparing To Fail"

In the software engineering world, I learnt to spend 30% of my time in planning, 30% in programming the website or software itself, and the remaining 30% in Testing.

I applied this to Google Ads, and through years of testing and developing campaigns, I have developed my own system.

The system is called "**The 7 Step Google Ads Blueprint System**" and is one that I currently use to manage a portfolio of almost $750,000.

I have personally gone through a lot of pain in "working things out". I've lost tens of thousands of pounds of my own hard-earned money by rushing into implementing what I thought would be a great Google Ads campaign. I learnt I needed to implement several steps. And I started implementing this into my campaigns. The more I implemented the better my Google Ads campaigns got. I started saving money for my clients, I started quickly producing results for my clients, and I started improving the return on ad spend for my clients (ROAS), until I figured out that hey, this is a system. A Blueprint that I have. This was then the birth of "The 7 Step Google Ads Blueprint System".

My system follows 7 Key steps:

1) **A**nalyse - Analysing the market

2) **A**udience – Identifying Target Audience

3) **A**im –Your Key Performance Indicators

4) **A**ccess – Prepare the website to convert visitors to customers

5) **A**ction – Build a highly optimised Google Ads campaign

6) **A**ugment - Optimising your Google Ads

7) **A**udit - Auditing & Reporting In line with business objectives

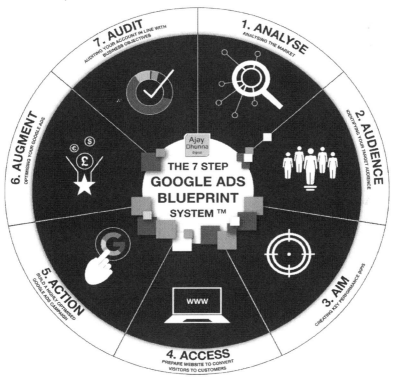

11) Getting the most out of this book

To help you get the most out of this book, and to understand how Google Ads works, I have compiled some of the basics you might like to consider. Here goes...

Theory vs Practice... Implementation Is Priceless!

Like all things, theory is one thing and practice is another. It's good to play around and experiment with the system within this book, whether you wish to start off from scratch, or even sit with someone who already manages Google Ads and ask them to show you around.

Whatever you decide, you can read all the books in the world, but what will really help you to best understand Google Ads, is implementation. Implementation is priceless, whether you do it yourself, or your team members, so that you can see for yourself, what the results are of what you have read and created.

Let me tell you, some of the best Google Ads experts I have trained up, I have done so by putting them into the deep end. Giving them a real project to work on. As a result, this demands real questions, not just textbook type Q&A's. Questions such as "Why this?", "Where do I do this from?". "How Do I?", "What Next? and "Oh Sh#te screwed up", and so on. And it's only by screwing up that you learn, you actually learn!

Create a Google Account as this book will show you. You don't necessarily have to use it. It will be just for practice purposes so that you can understand the items this book refers to.

On the other hand, if you only wish to know some of the main theories of what makes a successful and profitable Google Ads campaign, read at your leisure and I'm sure you will find bags of value and golden nuggets within this book.

Gmail

I would also suggest creating an email account with Google (Gmail). As we are primarily focusing on Google, creating an account with Google will enable you to access all platforms more easily, as well as integrations with one another more seamlessly.

To do this, go to www.gmail.com, and follow the prompts. By doing so you will have created an email address that you can use for all the Google platforms you use. For those of you who may be more tech-savvy, you can make your own email address into a Google email address too. Take your pick!

Take Your Time

What I find works best with me, as well as customers and students I speak to, is when they take in small amounts of information at a time. Maybe then couple this with the practical element, where they try out things that they have learned. I would therefore suggest the same process throughout this book. Read small amounts at a time, and try to implement what you may have learned, not necessarily on the Google platform, but even if it's making your own notes on how the advice and guidance given in this book, can be applied to your business.

Download the PPC Worksheet

I have created a worksheet which I use for all my Google Ads campaigns. Ensure to download it as we will be referring to it throughout this book.

The link is www.ajaydunna.com/ppcworksheet

12) Step 1 - Analyse

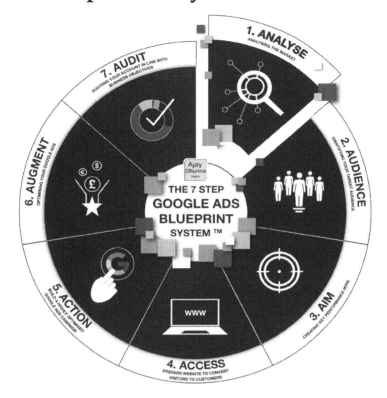

Here we analyse the market. Without conducting proper analysis, how will we ever know who we are competing against? How will we ever know how our products or services compare to theirs? We may think we have the best products in the world. But what is it that your competitors are putting out there, which could potentially be far superior to yours?

Here I will also introduce you to tools and templates I personally use and always have done, when implementing the Analysis stage prior to implementing a Google Ads campaign.

As humans, we sometimes get a little emotionally involved with our products or services, and start guarding it, thinking it's the best out there. And that's because we may have spent time building it. Lots of money maybe, sleepless nights. That's quite normal. But as a marketeer, it's imperative we step back and conduct detailed, objective market research, and detach yourselves from any emotions.

I once had a client, a dentist, who told me they want to market themselves as a general dentist, with a fairly low marketing budget. That was all well saying that. But when we looked around and conducted our analysis, we found they will just blend into the other local competitors, and there is nothing about them which stands out, as most of the local dentists were also general all-round dentists. It took some convincing to my client, but we then decided that based on the research we conducted, they need to be seen as an expert within orthodontics, in particular, Invisalign. We discovered a whole host of gaps in the market which our competitors were not taking advantage of. 6 months down the line, not only have we found the business turnover has increased by 20%, but people are travelling from all over the UK, not just the local area, primarily due to how we packaged up & marketed their services, standing out from the crowd, without having to compromise on price. In fact, once we have packaged up their services, it becomes a no-brainer for people to pay the price, regardless of where from the UK they travelled from.

Now when it comes to Google Ads, the importance of this amplifies. And that's because you are paying Google each time someone clicks on your Ads. And if the Ads are do not to convert into a lead or enquiries, your costs may go through the roof whilst your conversions remain low to none, or even non-profitable. This is why the Analysis stage is imperative, as it's helping to build a strong foundation for your Google Ads account.

So to help with this, I have outlined the main things you need to be aware of when analysing the market before implementing your Google Ads campaign.

These are the steps I take myself. Not only do these help me, to create a brilliant campaign which starts churning out leads and sales straight away, but these steps help my customers to better understand their own market, pricing, services, KPIs and so much more.

I also have a template which I use. This template helps me to keep my research well organised as well as constructive, so that I, or my clients, don't accidentally miss out on something important. This template really has been a gold mine for me. You can download it for free by visiting:

www.AjayDhunna.com/ppcTemplates

Competitors

This is a really interesting one. So many times, when I ask my customers, they end up giving me a huge list, and once I've finished with them, the list has shrunk to just one or two.

The reason is normally quite simple. There is a massive difference between who you "think" your competitor is and who is "actually" your competitor. Let me explain. So just because somebody sells the same products as you do or caters for the same services as you do does not necessarily make them a competitor, although technically they may be your competitor and you can learn from them.

Who I consider to be your competitors as far as online marketing is concerned are those that have a strong digital presence. In other words when you search on Google for their brand, their products, or services they are always there, predominantly towards the top of the search page. These are the companies who you are up against, when implementing a Google strategy for your business. Whether that be in the sponsored section at the top of the page, or the organic section (both of which we will cover later on).

So for example let's assume you are a chiropractor based in London. People who are looking for your products or services may well therefore, type into Google the words "chiropractor London", or "chiropractor near me". The question is: are the companies who you thought were your competitors anywhere to be found on the Google Search results page? If they cannot be found on the first page or even the second page for that matter then although they may be your competitor, I would not deem them to be your top three or four competitors to be concerned about or to even learn from.

The real threats are those who are listed on the first page or the second page but more so at the top of the first page, as they are the ones who are actively marketing their products and services which completed yours.

In many cases, the reason people sometimes think somebody is their competitor is because they may be getting lots of leads or sales. What you must understand is those people who may not be your competitor as far as Google is concerned, maybe your competitor on a different platform. In other words, they may be using different marketing strategies to get their leads and sales in the first place. For example, email nurturing, LinkedIn, Facebook, YouTube, Instagram, and the list goes on.

So why do we need to understand our competitors? By understanding our competitors:

    a) We can help to benchmark our business. We can identify gaps and opportunities in the market which we may be missing out on.

    b) Likewise, we can identify competing products or services. By understanding this, we can then dive deeper into how you can improve on this, have better messaging, stronger Ads, assess your pricing and so much more.

c) We can see what types of Ads they may be using to attract customers, which we can then model.

d) Similarly, we can research their landing pages to see how the landing pages have been setup, thereby utilising the things we learn from them.

How is this relevant to Google Ads? Simply put are gaining competitor intelligence to learn from their mistakes and to capitalise on the good work they may be doing.

Types of things you may want to look at are as follows:

Internal data

What do you know about your competitors? Brainstorm who you're likely to compete with and why. Ask yourself, what is it about specific competitors that make you think of them as competitors? Remember, in the digital world, your real competitors are arguably those that have a digital presence in terms of being shown on search engines, social media etc, for products or services that you also cater for.

Industry Research

What do you know about the wider industry? Who's an agitator? Who's "old faithful"? What's big on the horizon, which you can get in early on? A great tool I use for this is "Google Trends" which shows general search trends (trends.google.com). For example, using the word 'home office furniture' I can see clearly that this is an up-and-coming trend, within the date range and location specified. So, is this an indication of a service or product you may need to consider providing now and get in early?

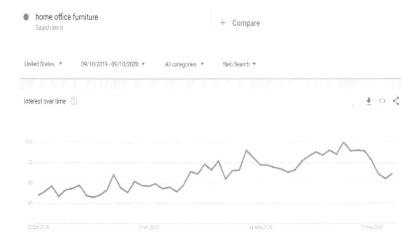

Do a search

Detach yourself from your business. You are the knowledge party within your business. Though this is good, it also means you're presumptuous. Presumptuous in that you may "think" people know what they are looking for, people know what they may be searching for. For example, I just typed the phrase:

"**Website top of google**".

Here you can see the intent of the searcher, it's clear that he wants to get his website listed at the top of Google. What it also shows is he may not be aware of technical terminology. So, this searcher is less likely to use words such as "Google Ads Specialist", or "Setting up a PPC account". If you were only marketing keywords which you know about and presumed your customers know about them, you would be missing out on potential business from customers who might be typing in keywords/phrases which are at a higher level.

Browsing and Retargeting

Retargeting is a way to show your advertisements to people who may have visited your website before but have now gone away from your website to another website altogether. Now here's a clever trick. Once you have researched your competitors, leave it a few days. When you are casually browsing other websites such as Facebook or content websites, you are likely to see their Ads, incentivising you to come back onto their website again. These are **retargeting Ads**. Take note of what types of Ads they are using, what page are they taking you to when you click on the Ad. All of a sudden, you have a new ammunition in your competitors' research basket.

We will be discussing retargeting in another module, so don't worry about it for now. But as a visual representation of how retargeting works, I have drawn a simple diagram:

[My Top Tip] – It's good to know the main difference between Retargeting & Remarketing. Retargeting is essentially focused on paid Ads, whereas Remarketing is more about using non-paid strategies such as email campaigns.

Researching & Forecasting

Accountabilities

Investigate who is responsible for what? Who is held accountable for budgeting? Who oversees performance? Consider completing a RACI (Responsible, Accountable, Consulted & Informed) of all areas and make sure you know who owns what! This help you get good insights into your competitors.

USPs

How can you shout about what you do and what makes you standout? In other words, what are your unique selling points that set you apart from your competitors? Consider what you can rely on to make you the one that wins the click!

Avoid thinking of the generic stuff which every tom-dick &
harry say i.e.

- We offer great service
- We have the best products on the market
- We pride ourselves
- Etc

However, something a little more tangible would be better.
For example:

- 30 day money back guarantee – no questions asked
- Next day delivery
- Free 30 minute consultation
- 2 year warranty
- ... I think you get the point!

Brand Guidelines

Is there anything you need to consider from a brand safety /
or guideline point of view? How should you talk about your
business, what tone of voice (TOV) should you be using?
What distinguishes your brand from your competitors? Use
your brand identity to draw engagement!

Customer Journey

Consider how the customer will interact with you and your
business. Don't forecast an immediate glut of sales if you
know it takes 4 weeks for the average sale to convert!
Higher-value products usually entail a longer-buying cycle.
Is there anything you can offer your customers at a lower
price entry? As a result, maybe you can then upsell them other

products or services. Can you provide a free demonstration of the product, either in person or online? Can you offer payment plans? What objections might your customer shave that you can address proactively?

By understanding your typical customers journey, you can make tweaks to your website as well as the ads you create, to significantly increase your conversion rate, otherwise known as conversion rate optimisation (CRO).

Keyword Research Like A Pro

Previously, we touched base on keyword research. Now let's start getting into the nitty-gritty. So, what is Keyword Research? According to Wikipedia,

> "Keyword research is a practice search engine optimization (SEO) professionals use to find and research search terms that users enter into search engines when looking for products, services or general information."

Though Wiki refers to SEO, we use the same type of process for Google Ads. I think Wiki needs to review their definition and open it up a little!

Using the right keywords will be one of the single most important decisions you will make that will determine how much you end up spending, how many conversions (leads or sales) you get, and more importantly, the quality of the leads you get.

It's also important to understand the simple concept of the less competitive keywords are, the lower CPCs (Cost-Per-Click) are on average. The opposite applies too, the more competitive the keywords are, the more you will usually end up paying per click.

Google's average CPC varies depending on many factors such as the industry you are in, the competitive nature of the service, competition, location, seasonal trends and so much more.

Before we move on, as and when we conduct research, keep exporting your keywords into a spreadsheet, with any data you have available for them. At a later date, we can then use this spreadsheet to use these within your Google Ads campaign.

You may also wish to download my free Google Ads Keywords template by visiting:
https://ajaydhunna.com/keywordtemplate

Keyword Funnel

I want to introduce you to the concept of "Keyword Funnel". A keyword funnel essentially helps you to categorize keywords depending on what stage a user is at. If we take a real-life example, let's say you were a salesperson at a Porsche car dealership, and 2 customers walked in. One asked "I want to buy a car" and the other asked, "I'd like to buy a Porsche Cayenne". If you were limited for time and had to serve just one of these customers, who would you serve? Most likely the 2nd one as the second customer is being more specific and you know you have more of a chance of converting them to a sale.

Keywords work in the same way, the more specific you are, the more you are likely to convert to a lead or sale.

In this example, the person who said "I want to buy a car" would be classified as higher up the Keyword Funnel, and the one who asked for "I'd like to buy a Porsche Cayenne" is lower down the funnel. You generally get a large number of searches/clicks for keywords that are higher up the funnel, and a lower number of clicks towards the bottom, but the ones at the bottom are more likely to convert.

See diagram below of how a keyword funnel may work, using illustrative figures which were true at the time of writing this book. As you can see, the keywords which are higher up the funnel, have a higher search volume (they are searched for a lot), their Cost Per Click is low, but their conversion rate is low (i.e., the quality of the keyword is low). In other words, the person using this keyword is at a fairly early stage within their sales journey, thus being higher up the funnel. In this case, they know they want to buy a Porsche but are not sure which one.

Likewise at the bottom of the funnel, i.e., Porsche Cayenne Dealer, though the search volume is low (Average 210 searches per month), the Average Cost Per Click Is Higher but the Conversion rate is far higher.

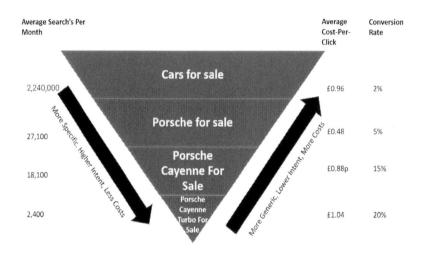

So what do we learn from this?

What we learn is to avoid only going for keywords which are higher up the keyword funnel, as though you may get a lot of clicks, the searcher is not quite yet ready to buy and is in "research phase".

Likewise avoid only going for just keywords which are at the bottom of the keyword funnel, as though you will get conversions, you will be missing out on opportunities whereby people may have conducted some high-level searches first, so now, they don't know who you are and are not aware of your brand.

Instead, implement a mixture of keywords that are at the top of the funnel and bottom, and adjust how much you are paying per click for each of these accordingly.

In terms of distribution, if you have a healthy budget, you can spread your budget across all levels of the keyword funnel. However, if you don't have an endless pot of money, bias your budget more so towards the mid to bottom of the funnel, as these keywords are more likely to drive you more conversions relatively quickly.

In this section, we will run through the steps I take to conduct competitor research. But before I do, I want to quickly cover the importance of your Categorising keywords.

Categorising Keywords

I always break keywords down into 3 categories. This helps me to better understand which keywords I'm ready to pay a fortune for, and those that I need to avoid at all costs, By categorizing your keywords into such categories could be the difference between instant success, or complete failure. What we are really trying to understand here is Keyword Intent. What is the Intent behind a keyword, which a user may type into Google? There are 2 main intents…

Research intent

These are keywords which people use to simply conduct research, with little or no intention to make a purchase or to enquire about a product or service.

For example:

- **"Best ways to cure anxiety myself"**
  Here, the user is clearly researching how to cure anxiety and wants to do it himself. As a result, the chances of this keyword converting into a lead or a sale is minimal.
- **"What is a good family car?".**
  Here, though the user seems to be at the research stage, it could be argued that they do have an intention to purchase. However, I would probably keep them into the research intent category as at this stage, they still have not seemed to have made up their mind as to the type of car they wish to buy and are very much at research stage.

Buying intent

These are keywords where the user clearly has a high intent to make a purchase or make an enquiry.

For example:

- **"local anxiety therapist"**
  This clearly shows this user is actively looking to hire the services of a local anxiety therapist. The chances of this keyword driving conversions is therefore much higher.

- **"4 x 4 Range Rover Sports Electric"**
  Here the user is being very specific and has more than likely already done his/her research as to what type of car they want, make, model, performance and fuel type.

Negative keywords

These are keywords which you want to ensure that your Ads on Google never show up, as you do not provide such services or projects.

Google works in a very funny way. You tell Google what keywords you want to be shown on, when a user conducts a search, and Google makes up its own mind, as to other close variations or synonyms it thinks the user might also be interested in. We must therefore tell Google that such keywords are not relevant to you or your business.

For example:

- "Garden decking jobs" - Here the intent of the user is to look for a job. You can then tell Google that if someone conducts a search, and if one of the words they type in is "job" or "vacancy or "apprentice" then we do not wish for our Ad to be shown. We would then put such keywords into a "Negative keyword list".

Steps For Putting Together Your Keywords

Step 1 - Brainstorm some keywords

In this step, we are first trying to find out "who" your online competitors are. There are so many ways you can do this, but what I have detailed is what we do and what works well for us.

Make a list of the core keywords which describe your services at a high level. These are also known as your "Seed Keywords". Put yourself in the shoes of a customer, what is it that you would type in to find your products or services?

- Cars
- Cars for sale
- Buy a car
- Porsche dealer
- Used Porsche for sale
- Porsche dealer near me
- Porsche dealer <Your location name> i.e. Porsche dealer London

Add these to your worksheet using the 'Keyword Intent' tab.

Step 2 - Let's see who are competing for these keywords

Now we wish to see who are the companies/websites that are competing for these keywords. There are many ways you can do this and many tools you can use. Now we will use the keywords you brainstorm in the earlier section, in one or more of the following keyword research tools. They all have their pros and cons, so I always suggest, try them all and see which one suits you best.

Here are a few ways:

Google

Go to Google.com, or Google.co.uk or whichever you prefer to use, and simply type one of your keywords. In this example, I typed in **USED PORSCHE FOR SALE** and the screenshot below shows what I can see, above the page-fold.

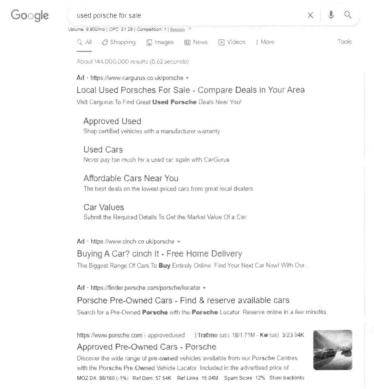

What you can see here is the advertisers who are competing in the Google Ads Auction, for the keyword "used Porsche for sale". In other words, these are advertisers/companies who are participating in the Google Ads platform auction, to be shown on Google for these keywords, which when clicked on, they will be charged a specific amount by Google, per click. Remember, the Google Ad listings are denoted by the "Ad" symbol, for example, see screenshot below:

Now although this is great as you can quickly get a snapshot of who is competing for the same keywords that you want to be found for, you don't get much more information than that. So, there is not a lot you can do with it from a Google Ads perspective.

This is where you can make a note of your competitors so that when conducting further research, you can quickly refer to them. Best way to do this is to use the worksheet, refer to the 'competitors' tab.

Tip:

Scroll to the bottom of the page. Here you will see a section titled "Searches related to...." and your keyword. This is where you can find some golden nuggets! Google is using the keyword you typed in, and is showing you other similar & related keywords, which people are commonly typing in. So now you are getting suggestions for keywords you might not even have thought about using.

Searches related to porsche dealer london

porsche **west** london   porsche **uk**
porsche **mayfair**   **used** porsche london
porsche **east** london   porsche **dealership**
porsche **dealers uk**   porsche **hatfield**

1   2   Next

This is where you can use various tools to help you get more information on your competitors. I will therefore discuss a few of the many tools I personally use.

Keyword Planner

Website link:

https://ads.google.com/home/tools/keyword-planner/

The Google Keyword planner is a free keyword research tool, and as its name implies, is owned by Google :-) By using Google keyword planner, you can quickly find out how many times keywords that are relevant to your business have been searched for, typically within the last 30 days.

More specifically Google Keyword planner allows you to:

1. Find out an estimate of how many times keyword have been recently searched (Called 'Search Volume').
2. Generate new keyword ideas by combining different keyword lists.
3. Create new keyword variations based on a primary keyword.
4. Provides Keywords used on specific websites which is excellent for competitive analysis.

Using Google planner is free. However, in order to use Google Keyword Planner, you need to have:

1. A Google Ads account. Note this does not need to be active.
2. Have at least 1 Google Ads campaign created.
3. If you have created a Google Ads account and have not yet entered your billing details and got an active campaign running, you may still use Google Keyword Planner, but the data Google will show for search volumes, will be broader.

The screenshot below shows what the Keyword Planner looks like when you first log into it.

Here you will get 3 areas:

> 1) **Discover new Keywords**. This is where you can type some keywords which you feel people might search for when looking for your business, and Google will give you some statistics on.
>
> 2) **Get search volume and forecasts**. Here Google will give you some forecasting information, allowing you to get an idea of how many conversions (Leads/Sales) you are likely to get for a specific budget, what your average cost may be etc.
>
> 3) **Plans created for you**. Whatever keywords you research, you will be able to see a summary of them within this section.
>
> In this example, I typed in 3 keywords:
> - Cars for sale
> - Porsche for sale
> - Porsche dealer

See table below what Google Keyword planner shows

Keyword (by relevance)	↓	Vol	CPC	Comp	Trend	Avg. monthly searches	Competition	Top of page bid (low range)	Top of page bid (high range)
Keywords that you provided									
porsche for sale ☆		27,100	£0.43	0.33		3,600	Medium	£0.09	£0.43
cars for sale ☆		2,240,000	£0.94	0.46		246,000	High	£0.25	£0.94
porsche dealer ☆		40,500	£3.21	0.09		2,900	Low	£0.48	£2.28

So what does all this in the table above mean? Let me explain in a semi-layman's way:

1) **Keyword that typed in**:

   This column shows the keywords you typed in.

2) **Volume**:

   Shows on average, how many times the keyword you typed in, has been recently searched for, within the location and date range specified.

3) **CPC**:

   This is the Average Cost-Per-Click you can expect to pay, each time someone searches for these keywords and clicks on the ads.

4) **Comp** and **Competition**:

   The Comp column shows how competitive this keyword is, and ranges from 0 to 1.0 (Typical of Google not to use a simple 1 to 10 system instead :-)). In the "Competition" column, you can see the same information, except represented by High, Medium or Low. The more advertisers that compete for visibility, the higher the competition.

5) **Trend**:

   Now, I love this column! As it shows a summary of how many times this keyword has been searched for over recent months. Using this can tell you a lot about the seasonal impact of the keyword. You can either just look at the graph to get a quick summary, or if you hover over it, a small window will open showing you monthly search volumes.

6) **Avg. Monthly Searches**:

This shows on average, how many people have searched for this keyword, within your target location and date range.

7) **Top of page bid (low range) and Top of page bid (high range)**:

This gives us an idea of how much we may need to bid, for our ads to show above the organic search results on Google.

Wait! It gets better. Scroll down the page a little… The Google Keyword Planner tool will now also give you keywords ideas, based on your original set, which you may also like to consider using.

Keyword ideas								
☐ carsales ★	1,500,000	£0.39	0.01		4,400	Low	£0.25	£0.85
☐ used cars ★	1,220,000	£1.55	0.56		110,000	High	£0.33	£0.96
☐ used cars for sale ★	823,000	£1.45	0.72		90,500	High	£0.32	£0.88
☐ bmw m4 ★	823,000	£0.76	0.08		49,500	Low	£0.17	£0.52
☐ used cars near me ★	17,000	£1.90	0.55		18,100	Medium	£0.38	£1.19
☐ cars for sale near me ★	450,000	£1.32	0.56		135,000	Medium	£0.23	£0.78
☐ car dealerships near .. ★	823,000	£3.34	0.29		74,000	Medium	£0.64	£2.74

The brilliant thing is you can now tick the boxes for the keywords you are interested in, click ADD KEYWORDS and they will be added to your "plan" which we discussed earlier. Here you can see some forecasting and trend information, based on all the keywords you have added. You may also add the keywords you have selected into an existing campaign.

So for example, using the keywords you added, you can see some forecasting information. In this case, I wanted to see how much traffic I can get if I were to bid an average of £1.50 per click, for the next 7 days. What The Plan is telling me is if I were to go all-out, it would cost me £4,100, if my conversion rate was 5%, I could receive 220 conversions. If my conversion Value was £1,500, it means i have had 320,000 worth of conversions. Needless to say, you can specify your own daily budget and not go along with what Google suggests.

Create Charts

At the top of the page, you will notice you can see an overview chart which shows trends for the keywords you have entered.

This may look something like this:

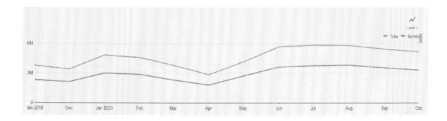

Note: if you click on the CHART icon, you can get different data such as typical device usage, or User Locations.

Now that we have an idea of keywords, we can similarly get data on keywords used by competitors. Similar to the way we have conducted keyword research, click Discover new keywords, then, instead click on START WITH A WEBSITE and simply enter your competitor's website address as per screenshot below. Click GET RESULTS and you will get a similar data to the one I showed you above. Isn't that fantastic!

Conclusion about Google's Keywords Planner tool

Great tool. Shame it requires you to have a Google Ads account prior to using it. But it's a great starter, and it's free to use. I have found that though we get to see estimates on trends, search volumes, average cost-per-click etc, the data you see must be treated with caution, as it is only a guide, and not always accurate. The only way to get accurate data, is by implementing the campaigns in Google Ads.

Once you have found your keywords, add them into your worksheet, within the 'our researched keywords' tab. This is the ideal place to also take note of additional information such as search volumes, estimates cost per click etc.

SEMrush

SEMrush is a paid tool, which allows you to conduct various types of research for SEO (Search Engine Optimisation), Paid Advertising and so much more. But for the sake of this book, we will only focus on Paid Advertising.

I won't go through all the usual metrics now, as I have covered them within the Google Planner section.

The concept is pretty much the same, we enter a competitor, and SEMrush gives you competitor data. SEMrush calls their equivalent tool, "**Advertising Research Tool**".

Ad	Keyword	Pos.	Diff.	Block	Volume	CPC (USD)	URL	Traffic	Traffic %	Costs (USD)
🔲	autotrader	1 → 1	0	🔲	5,000,000	0.61	https://www.yes... com/uk/ 🔗	235,000	58.04	143.4K
🔲	cars for sale	1 → 1	0	🔲	246,000	0.54	https://www.yes... .com/uk 🔗	11,562	2.85	6.2K
🔲	cars for sale near me	1 → 1	0	🔲	135,000	0.46	https://www.yes... ed-cars 🔗	6,345	1.56	2.9K
🔲	cars for sale near me	1 → 1	0	🔲	135,000	0.46	https://www.yes... .com/uk 🔗	6,345	1.56	2.9K
🔲	gumtree cars	1 → 1	0	🔲	110,000	0.48	https://www.yes... .com/uk 🔗	5,170	1.27	2.5K
🔲	gumtree cars	1 → 1	0	🔲	110,000	0.48	https://www.yes. . 5002345 🔗	5,170	1.27	2.5K
🔲	used cars	1 → 1	0	🔲	110,000	0.60	https://www.yes... .com/uk 🔗	5,170	1.27	3.1K

Here you can see an example of the sort of table SEMrush show. As you can see it shows more data on the right, where it breaks down individual keywords, so you can get a breakdown of specific keywords which SEMrush gives you ideas on. So, I'm not going to bore you with the same details, as generally, the principles are the same.

However in addition you get additional information such as:

Competitor Position Roadmap

This is where you can visualise who your main competitors are at a glance:

A feature I like in SEMrush is it shows you a tabular summary of the overlap between keywords you are advertising, and they are advertising. See "Comp Level" column. It shows in this case, if you look at CINCH.CO.UK, there are for example 314 common keywords (when compared to your keywords) and they have a total of approximately 1,600 Paid keywords, all of which you can export into a spreadsheet, and decide which of those you may wish to use too, within your Google Ads campaign!

Paid Competitors 1 - 100 (275)

Domain	Com. Level	Common Keywords	Paid Keywords
cinch.co.uk	20%	314	1.6K
cazoo.co.uk	12%	137	753
cargurus.co.uk	10%	106	504
volkswagen.co.uk	4%	63	1.3K
kia.com	4%	58	1.3K
autotrader.co.uk	4%	39	592

This is where things really start getting interesting, and the value of using a paid tool really starts to kick in! SEMrush also shows you the actual Ads your competitors are using and as well as which Ads keywords are being used for each of these Ads.

Ad Copies 1 - 100 (489) *i*

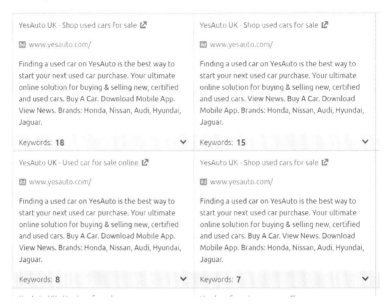

By analysing Ads which your competitors are using, you can start evaluating things like:

o   Which Ads have been receiving the most amount of clicks

o   How long the ads have been used for

o   The ad copy which is being used

o   Landing pages used

o   Etc.

You can then start using this information to model your own ads by improving on them.

UberSuggests

Ubersuggest does pretty much what the Google Keyword Planner and SEMrush do. It is certainly worth using as I find using multiple tools, gives me a clearer picture of competitors, keyword ideas and so much more. You can also use Ubersuggest for free for a period of time which give you limited data. If you like it, consider signing up for a paid version to take advantage of the full data it provides you.

One cool feature I absolutely love about Ubersuggest is it provides you with Keyword intent data. Its "Keyword Magic" tools break keywords into the following:

- Information Keywords
- Commercial Keywords
- Navigational Keywords
- Transactional Keywords

Google Trends

Google Trends is one of my favourite tools. Most decisions I make are data-driven decisions. When I get a customer telling me they have the coolest product or service in the world, which no one has yet tapped into, Google Trends is one of the tools I quickly tap into, to see if what they are telling me carries any weight, or am I going to have to be the bearer of the bad news!

Google trends allow you to quickly see a graph showing you trends for a particular search term/keyword. This can be broken down to a specific country or year. In other words, it can show you the demand for a search term or keyword over a period of time. As a result, you can quickly gauge if whatever you are searching for, has an upward trajectory or a declining one. If upwards, then how sharp is the trajectory and has it hit its peak?

Check out the graph below for the word 'electric cars', location - worldwide, timespan - 5 years. It clearly shows a continuous growth in demand and is constantly increasing. By looking at this graph alone, you can gain some degree of confidence that the demand for electric cars, is yet to increase, and I wouldn't be surprised to see a spike in demand either!

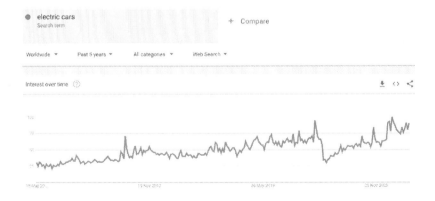

13) Step 2 - Audience

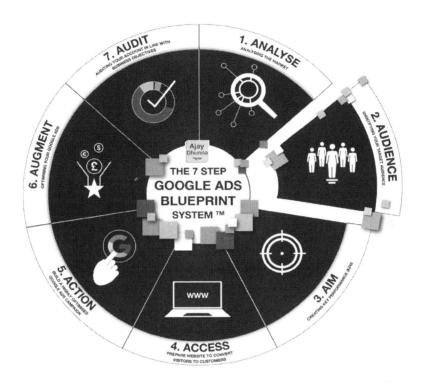

It is essential to know who we are trying to target. Who are our target audiences? Here, I will help you to understand what the audience is and why it is crucial to define your target audience from day dot!

Understanding Your Audiences & Avatars

Targeting audiences is one of marketing's earliest concepts. Understanding and appealing to your customer's needs is the best way to drive sales. One of digital marketing's significant benefits is that it substantially simplifies targeting; there is now a wealth of available marketing data, both historical and real-time, so it makes sense to exploit it. For instance, there are numerous Google tools within the Google Digital marketing Toolbox along with various third party real-time data platforms such as Lotame and Funnel.

Here we will look at the science and art of targeting customers, including getting to know your existing customers (audience analysis) and extending this to other groups to attract potential buyers from different sectors.

We will introduce the concept of "avatars" in marketing and show why this is highly effective in segmenting our audience and fine-tuning customer targeting. We will show how this is compatible with Google Ads targeting and observation modes.

What is a Customer Avatar?

The word "avatar" has many connotations that range from the earthly manifestation to a hybrid creature with a mix of human and alien DNA. We use avatars in video games and social media. But here, in the context of digital marketing, we are using an avatar, or preferably several avatars, as the embodiment of our perfect customer. So why don't we say, "target audience?"

The reason is subtle. When we think of target audiences, we tend to think in terms of averages. We group many potential buyers and take the mean. For instance, if we are selling clothes, we would discover that the average dress size in the UK is size 15, the figure provided by YouGov. However, the ideal dress size is considered size 11 for 18 to 39-year-old women, 13 for those aged 40 to 59, and 14 for women aged 60 and over.

You can think of a customer avatar as a persona that is imbued with carefully crafted characteristics. Each avatar will represent your perfect customer in the targeted niche. With this approach, we can be far more granular in targeting our customers. We can assign multiple avatars, each with its unique characteristics.

For instance, our avatars may be characterised by gender (sex), age, marital status, motivations, aspirations, interests, household income, and so forth for our clothing store. We would then serve the most relevant ads to those who would be more likely to take an interest in them. This approach avoids wasting money serving ads that fall wide of the mark and would likely be ignored.

Building Avatars

The easiest way to construct avatars is to use a template or multiple templates. You can start with the example below and modify it, or you may wish to create your own. Begin by developing a set of questions that will help you understand your perfect customer. For instance:

Name	It's a good idea to create a name. Let's say *Pam*	Your Notes
Demographics	Age	
	Gender	
	Occupation	
	Education	
	Income	
	Marital status	
	Parental status	
Work-life	Job title	
	What is their role?	
	How do they influence their work environment	
	What motivates them?	
	Work frustrations	
	Career aspirations	

Personality	Introvert, extrovert, balanced?	
	Political leaning	
	IQ and EQ characteristics	
	Pain points	
	Sociability etc.	
Lifetime goals	What motivates them?	
	Short and long time aspirations	
	Aspirations for their children	
	A bigger house?	
	A new car?	
	A luxury round-the-world cruise?	

These are just a few examples; you will undoubtedly be able to come up with more. By the time you have finished, you should understand *Pam* and know what makes her tick. You can then do another one addressing her big brother *John*.

By building your avatars you can then adjust various factors of your Google Ads campaigns. For example:

- The ad copy you use can be tailored to your avatar.
- Your demographics i.e., you might decide to target a specific gender or age range.
- Locations – by understanding your avatar, you can adjust your location targeting to only serve ads within those locations.
- Interests – you can overlay your targeting to include interests as well as keywords.

You can refer to the "avatar" tab within your worksheet to help you build your avatars.

14) Step 3 - Aim

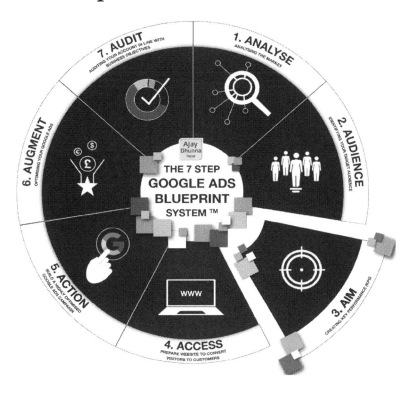

Here we figure out what we are actually aiming to achieve. What we don't want to do is to start marketing campaigns until we understand the maths of exactly what statistics we are trying to achieve, our KPIs, our budgets and so on. For this, we use the "Aim" stage within "The 7 Step Google Ads Blueprint System".

Budgeting

Intro on budgeting

Most businesses I speak to don't have a limitless budget to spend on marketing. I say that with a hint of sarcasm. It's funny, when I go to see companies who wish to engage with us to implement their marketing strategies, when asked, "What's your marketing budget?", you can bet that 9 out of 10 say, "We don't have one, tell us what it will take". It is almost like they feel we're going to take all their hard-earned pennies and take a trip to the South of France to sip away at the finest wine! Interestingly, when we do come back with a budget, then the normal answer is, "it's too high", or "this isn't within our budget" or "what can we do for a lower budget?" in the words.

it's not that they didn't have the budget, because they clearly did, they would not have been asking us to reduce, but the mere fact is they just did not want to disclose it.

So let me tell you one thing,

Marketing campaigns can range from as little as $10 a day to 10s of 1000s of dollars a day.

So the question is, what is it that you can afford, within your budget, so that when the marketing company does come back to you?

The proposals that they come back with fall in line with your budgets, and you're not in for a nasty shock.

And the flip side, when they do come back to you.

It's not the case that their proposal is way under what you otherwise would have been ready to expend so have a budget in mind.

Whether the budget is, for the first month, the first quarter. The year. And don't be afraid to tell the marketing company what your budget is.

Because only by doing so, can your agency come back with a proposal, which meets your financial constraints. Only then can you work well with your marketing experts to help meet your needs and objectives. By better understanding your budget, your agency can create a more strategic plan of how they can help you to accomplish your goals, which may entail a hybrid strategy using multiple various channels.

If you are considering using Google Ads for your business, you will need to know how much it will cost you and the potential benefits. The accepted wisdom is that small businesses should spend between 5% and 12% of their revenue on marketing, but that is far from being a firm rule. The amount you spend will depend on many factors, including the maturity of your company, the sector you operate in, and your short-term objectives. For instance, if you want to reach a large audience quickly, you might aim to splash out on an extensive marketing campaign at the outset before establishing a steady revenue stream. Whatever your situation, adding Google Ads to your marketing channels is likely to provide positive results.

When it comes to how much you should spend on Google Ads, there is, of course, no firm answer out there. "As long as a piece of string" comes to mind. But here we will try to provide a little guidance to help you decide. First, we will quickly review how Google Ads operates and then drill down to some more pithy material on the key metrics you should focus on. We will say a few words on modelling and optimising your Google Ads campaigns and an example of how to allocate your initial budget.

How Google Ads makes money

To recap, Google Ads is, of course, Google's advertising platform where businesses bid to show ads on search results pages and websites. It is the principal income earner for Alphabet, Google's holding company. There is also a Google Shopping channel, but we will look at that in detail on another occasion. For now, we will focus on Google Ads.

Advertisers can choose whether their ads will appear on search engines' results pages (the Google Search Network), on websites, apps, and videos (the Google Display Network) or both. Advertisers pay Alphabet based on a pay-per-click (PPC) basis for search ads, but there are alternative ways to pay for display ads. For instance, you can pay on a CPM basis (cost-per-thousand impressions) which is recommended if you want to increase your visibility or stick with PPC. Google also offer a CPC model (cost per conversion).

Budgeting basics

It is essential to realise that you do not pay for ad impressions with PPC; you are only charged when somebody clicks on your ad. What is important is how much that click will cost you - your cost per click (CPC); how frequently people will click on your ad - the click-through rate (CTR); and what proportion of those clicks will result in you achieving your objective – the conversion rate (CR).

It is a little more complicated than that. Google is secretive about precisely how its algorithm works. You might think from the above that there is little point in a small business participating, as larger enterprises will entirely dominate the scene. But that's not the case. Google encourages the participation of small businesses, and the algorithm ensures that they get a fair deal. From experience, we can state categorically that Google Ads can work very well for a small business.

Key Google Ads metrics

We have already mentioned the three metrics you should focus on to set your budget. These are the cost per click (**CPC**), click-through rate (**CTR**), and conversion rate (**CR**). We will now look at these in detail. The actual values that you experience will be specific to your campaign, but we can learn much by looking at averages for different industry sectors.

You will see significant differences between the various industries and the cost and performance of search and display ads.

Cost per Click (CPC)

The first chart shows the average CPC across multiple sectors for both search and display networks. The figures are in dollars as they are based on US data which are bigger and more readily available than UK data. However, it is a reasonable approximation to the UK. Note the difference between the search (left hand) and display (right hand) scales.

In all sectors, the display CPC is less than one dollar. Law and Government have the highest CPC (over $6) and Dining and Nightlife the lowest (just over $1). If you are working in one of these or a closely related sector, you can see what your CPC might be.

Click-Through Rate (CTR)

You won't be charged for an ad impression' you will only be charged when somebody clicks on it. But you do need to know the probability that your ad will be clicked on. If you have a high CTR and a high CPC, you will likely burn through your budget quickly. If that is the case, you will probably need to focus your ad on your target audience more closely. The following graphic shows average CTRs for various sectors.

Here it is interesting to note that there tends to be an inverse relationship between CTR and CPC. For instance, Law and Government have a high CPC and low CTR, while Dining and Nightlife have a low CPC and a high CTR. Again, you can get some idea of the CTR for your sector.

Conversion Rate (CR) (or Conversion rate Value (CRV)

Your CR is critically important. It is the proportion of visitors who click on your ad and go on to complete your desired goal—for instance, making a purchase or signing up for a newsletter. If your CR is high, you are doing well, and your Google Ads campaign is working for you. If it is low, then you should do something about improving it, or your campaign might cost you more than it brings in. Here are the average CRs across the various sectors.

Vehicles would appear to have the highest CR closely followed by Law and Government. Apparel is a highly competitive sector. From the above, you can see the kind of CR you should aim for.

Modelling and Optimising Your Google Ads Campaign

Now that you are armed with the key metrics, you will need to optimise your campaign. Don't expect to achieve all your goals from the start. You will almost certainly need to modify a range of parameters before reaching your goals, always keeping a close eye on the metrics we have highlighted. The overall aim is to reduce your costs and maximise your ROI.

The elements of your model should be:

1) Selection of keywords and phrases – this is critical, and we recommend that you do extensive research on the subject

2) Ad design – this is harder than it seems and may take several iterations to get right

3) Excluding keywords that have a low CR and are costing you money without reward

4) Geolocating your campaign to exclude pointless clicks for people who geographically can't take advantage of what you are offering

5) Optimise the design of your landing pages. Good landing pages will increase your CR

6) Continuously monitor and analyse your results

An example of a starter budget

While your budget will depend on your sector and your specific business environment, this example should provide you with a starting position that you can build on. We will use PPC search ads to keep it simple, but you can apply the same principles for display ads.

Step 1 – Allocate a total marketing budget

Let's assume your business generates a revenue of **$500,000** pa. Allocating 10% of this to marketing means your total marketing spend should be around £50,000.

Step 2 – Setting your initial Google Ads budget

Naturally, you will be using a range of marketing channels, but it's not unusual for businesses to spend 40% to 50% of this on Google Ads, so lay you will allocate a ceiling of $24,000 a year, or **$2,000 a month**. The beauty of Google Ads is that you don't need to make a long-term commitment. It is best to set a monthly budget and iterate on this, depending on the results.

Step 3 – Estimate the CPC for your keywords

Your actual CPC is the total cost of your campaign divided by the total number of clicks. However, we will start by using the average CPC figures given above. Let's say you operate in the Computer and Related sector, where the average CPC is $2.8. Note that the average CTR is 3.5% for this sector, and the average CR is 3.2%.

Step 4 – Set your target revenue and ROI

The big question is, how much is a conversion worth to you in terms of profit? Your conversion could be part of a multi-channel purchase decision, or it could be as simple as making a purchase. For simplicity, let's say it is a purchase that will generate $1,000 revenue with a profit of $200.

You also need a target ROI. The ROI on PPC tends to be higher than alternative marketing channels, so you might wish to target an ROI of 100%; in other words, for each $1 you spend on Google Ads, you aim to generate $2 profits.

Step 5 – Putting it all together

Your target spend is $2,000 a month, and you aim to generate a profit of $4,000 on sales of $20,000. Thus, you need 20 conversions. Given a conversion rate of 3.2%, you will need (100/3.2) x 20 clicks = 625 clicks.

A CPC of $2.8 would involve an initial outlay of $625 x 2.8 = $1,750, which is well within your budget, leaving a reasonable contingency. However, if your return per click were much less than these figures, you would fall short of your targets.

Step 6 – Setting your minimum ROI per click

An alternative approach is deciding the minimum profit you need to generate per click to make PPC worthwhile. For instance, using the same parameters, each $2.8 (CPC) you spend will generate 3.2/100 (CR) = 0.032 conversions. Thus, to break even, each conversion must generate a profit of $87.5 and, to make a 100% ROI, it must generate $175. In other words, CPC x CR.

Finally

If you came here to find out how much a Google Ads campaign might cost you, we have already done the "how's long a piece of string" routine. It all depends, and we have indicated many of the things on which it depends. However, if it helps, a large corporation might spend over $50 million a year on Google Ads, while a small business might budget between $1,000 to $10,000 a month.

A great approach is to dive in at the start with your best-calculated guess and then constantly review your returns and budgets, optimising as you go. Never be scared to reallocate budgets based on what is generating the best profits. Always have a backup plan and be patient. If ROI is falling below expectations, try to revise your strategy before abandoning it. With Google Ads, you are in control, so make the best of it.

If you would like to get more information about your proposed campaign, please get in touch. We would be happy to hear from you.

To help you get a very vague indication as to what conversion rates in your industry may be, here's a screenshot I took from Wordstream.com:

Industry	Average CVR (Search)	Average CVR (GDN)
Advocacy	1.96%	1.00%
Auto	6.03%	1.19%
B2B	3.04%	0.80%
Consumer Services	6.64%	0.98%
Dating & Personals	9.64%	3.34%
E-Commerce	2.81%	0.59%
Education	3.39%	0.50%
Employment Services	5.13%	1.57%
Finance & Insurance	5.10%	1.19%
Health & Medical	3.36%	0.82%
Home Goods	2.70%	0.43%
Industrial Services	3.37%	0.94%
Legal	6.98%	1.84%
Real Estate	2.47%	0.80%
Technology	2.92%	0.86%
Travel & Hospitality	3.55%	0.51%

https://www.wordstream.com/blog/ws/2016/02/29/google-adwords-industry-benchmarks

Define Your KPIs

What do you want from the Google Ads account you are creating? Like how many sales, or what should the value of sales be which you wish to achieve, and within what period of time? Or if it is the leads you are looking for, then exactly how many? Are you looking for an efficient ROAS? Or maybe you are focused on acquiring a consistent Cost-Per-Acquisition (CPA). Make sure you know what you're budgeting for.

It is imperative you keep these as realistic as possible.
Some will want brand awareness - focus on traffic.
Some will want leads - focus on quality,
Whilst e-commerce businesses may wish to focus on ROAS (Return On Ad Spend).
Think both short and long-term. If you already have existing campaigns and data, then it makes working out your KPIs a lot easy.

Not only is it important to know what metric you are going to use, but also what values are you going to associate with those metrics.

Here are a few examples…

Example 1
Maybe you have a web design agency and are looking to achieve leads. In which case you are more likely going to want to focus on Conversions as well as CPA.

Let's assume on average a CPC (Cost-Per-Click) is $5 and on average it takes 20 clicks to get 1 conversion. Your actual CPA is therefore 5 x 20 = $100. You can now use this data-driven approach to set a new CPA, which as discussed earlier should be in the region of a maximum of 10 to 15% reductions. In the can you can adjust the Google bid settings to target a CPA of $85 and monitor its conversion rates and cost per conversion at the same time over a period of time.

[My Top Tip] Let's not get too ambitious. When adjusting Target CPA, maybe do increments of 10% at a time and allow the algorithm to settle down for a good few weeks before you determine if it has worked or not.

Example 2

Using the same scenarios as above, let's say you are not overly bothered about CPA but just want as many leads as possible. In this case, you can set your bid strategy to 'Maximise conversions' only, in which case the algorithm will drive as many potential conversions as possible, without factoring in CPA.

Consider Seasonality

Should you split your budget evenly through the year? Or do you need to work around key industry peaks and times? Consider Christmas, School Holidays, Summer etc. Demands for your services may be more, or less competitive depending on the seasonality so it is worth reviewing targets respectively.

When are People Shopping vs Buying?

Do you have a long consideration time? Does it take a while for people to buy? If so, factor in that people may wish to visit your website several times before they make a purchase, in which case you could even consider allocating a budget for retargeting.

How does your finance process work?

Is there anything you need to consider internally - are you limited to a weekly budget etc?

Do you want to Grow, or Maintain?

Is your objective to get bigger quick - or are you looking to re-invest gently? Consider phasing and constraints to your cash flow. Maybe set your budgets Quarterly instead of a blanket monthly budget for the whole 12 months.

15) Step 4 - Access

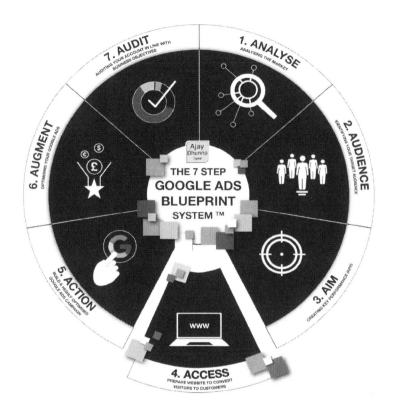

By Access, I mean, what is it that people are going to get access to, once they have clicked on Google, to access your information about your products or services? 9 times out of 10, this would be your website!

Wow, "website"! I remember back in 1996 when I set up my first ever business, Web-Tech. And this is the screenshot of the homepage of my first ever website. Geeze, how much things have changed!

109

Back in those days, we used to ask people, "Do you want a static website or a dynamic one (i.e., database driven)?" And we really had to go to town to explain the differences of what these are. Static websites would be built using only hand-coded HTML and maybe a bit of JavaScript, which if they wanted some changes done to, they will have to come to us and we will charge them, though the initial costs will be lower. On the other hand, dynamic websites, as we called them were "database driven" websites that would be built using a "server-side" programming language such as ASP, or PHP as it were in those days, allowing our customers to log in and make as many changes as you want without incurring additional expenses!

It's amazing when talking about website domain names, these days we say ".co.uk" or ".com" whereas back in the days, people used to say "full stop c, o full stop u. k" and "full stop c,o,m"! Look how far time has come in just over 2 decades. It frightens me to think about what lies ahead in another decade's time, let alone 2 decades' time. Anyway, I just had a few flashbacks whilst starting this chapter which I needed to get off my chest.

Anyway, the point being is that things change and technology changes. Consumer expectations change, as does consumer knowledge, demands, trends and so much more. I generally find that every 4-5 years, there are always some big shifts in technology, and it is our job to keep up to date with them and those that don't, fail, and fail hard.

With that in mind, here's what I feel works well... **today**!

The most critical element in any digital marketing project is your website. The primary aim in almost all Google Ads campaigns is to send your audience there, so it's essential to provide your visitor with the best possible experience you can create for them. Your website is your one opportunity to grab your visitors' attention and convert them into paying customers.

But what makes a good website? Of course, there is no definitive answer. Hardly anybody gets it right from the start. Websites tend to evolve as their designers continually make changes to optimise their performance; however, there are several essential elements that all good websites have in common, so let's focus on these.

Just to put this into perspective, according to internet live statistics, there are over 1.8 billion websites online right now, so there is plenty of data out there we can learn from.

From a Google Ads perspective, it is essential that when people click on an ad, they are taken to the most relevant page on your website. Avoid taking people to the home page as you are they relying on them to navigate around your website, which reduces conversion rates. If your ad is about "Plumbers in Birmingham", then hey, take people to a page which is related to plumbers in Birmingham. This is widely known as a 'landing page'.

What makes a good landing page website?

1.   Your website satisfies users' needs

Far too many websites put themselves first and set out to showcase the owner's business. Unfortunately, this approach is a little like putting the cart before the horse; in other words, it's the wrong way around. Instead, good websites focus primarily on the customer and solve their pain, wants, needs, and dilemmas.

You need to understand your audience and what they want. Does what you provide to your visitors improve at least some aspects of their life? The story you tell should align with what your customers want to achieve.

Remember that your visitors are focused on their own goals and unlikely to have the time or the inclination to read or view content that fails in this role. In addition, ensure that your content is unique to your website and not plagiarised from another source. While the way Google handles duplicate content is relatively complex and using it might or might not incur a penalty, duplicate content is best avoided.

This holistic design ethos applies to every aspect of your website, including most of the elements we describe below. They should all work in harmony to create the ultimate user experience that satisfies your visitors rather than adding to their frustration.

So ask yourself, does your landing page give enough information to your users to make them feel that you have the answer to their requirements? Or are you spending far too long babbling on about how great you are and how your grandfather built the business up 20 years ago!

2.   Fast loading

Few things are more frustrating than websites that take a long time to load. Pages with load times longer than a few seconds will lose your visitors quickly. Optimising your pages for speed will enhance your user experience and potentially improve your search engine ranking. Some of the factors that impact loading speed include the number of images, videos and other media files; plugins and themes; coding and server-side scripts. An excellent tool to check your loading speed is Google PageSpeed Insights (https://pagespeed.web.dev/)

3.   Excellent design and user interface

Excellent design includes far more than making your website look beautiful. While looking good is an important feature, it is far more vital to satisfy your users' goals. Therefore, the messages you provide must be clear and concise, easy to navigate, and uncluttered. Unfortunately, now that we all have fast broadband, there is a tendency for many designers to use ever more cluttered designs that do nothing to enhance user experience. This is a case of "less is more"; simple, straightforward typography, imagery, and navigation, will make it easy for your visitors.

Understanding how users read websites is also critical. There are various design paradigms based on this, and one of the more popular of these is the "F" layout. Eye-tracking studies have established that most people read their screens following an "F" pattern, so the paradigm suggests that you should place the most important design elements on the left side.

4.   Trustworthy, safe & secure

We cannot overemphasise how crucial it is to make your website trustworthy, safe and secure. Sites that fail in this are quickly identified as such by search engines, and users are now warier than ever about visiting websites that fail to live up to high safety standards. You also run a serious risk that someone might hack your website and destroy your reputation. The fundamental security standards your website should adhere to include:

- HTTPS protocol assures your visitors they are interacting with the correct server and that their session is safe from interception. If you fail to use this, your web browser will likely identify your site as "not secure". Secure sites display a padlock to the left of the URL in your browser.
- SSL – secure sockets layer certificate – this means that the communication between your user's browser and the server is encrypted and thus cannot be hacked.
- GDPR policies – when handling sensitive user information, you are legally obliged to adhere to General Data Protection Regulations (GDPR). Therefore, your website should include a clear statement of your privacy policy, explaining how you use customers' data. Search engines are likely to de-rank your site if they fail to locate your privacy statement.

5.   Social media friendly

Social media is a crucial element of marketing, so your website should integrate with modern social media. Doing so makes it easier for your visitors to share important information with their particular social networks. This has the potential to increase your audience substantially with a positive impact on your search ranking. Some ways in improving your social media friendliness include:

- Create content that people want to share. Is your content beneficial and solves problems in a novel way? Are you a thought leader in your chosen niche? Are your graphics excellent and original?

- Make your content easily shareable. Of course, the first step is to produce content that people want to share, but you should also make it easy for them to do so, for instance, by including sharing button that provides single-click sharing.

- Include live chat. Live chat has the potential to engage your customers immediately and build rapport. While live chat is resource-hungry and not always possible, if you have sufficient resources to monitor and respond to messages, it can be very worthwhile.

6.   Search engine friendly

It is essential to distinguish between creating a search engine-friendly website (SEF) and search engine optimised (SEO). While both are important, SEF focuses on making it easy for search robots to navigate and understand your website. To be SEF, your website should:

Have 100% valid coding - always validate your HTML and CSS coding. Doing so will ensure that it is compatible with all web browsers and that search engines will accurately interpret the code and decipher the content.

- Accurate page titles – every page should have a valid title. Note that the page title will appear in search engine results pages (SERP).

- Proper heading tags – always use proper heading tags <h1>, <h2>, <h3> etc.
- Links – use valid links with appropriate anchor text.
- Meta-tags – these are important for search engines.
- ALT tags – ensure that every image on your website has an ALT tag that describes the image.
- CSS – nowadays, it almost goes without saying that you should use a CSS design – but not everybody does.

7.   Optimised for mobile

Every website should be optimised for mobile. The best approach is to think "mobile-first"; in other words, design your site for the smallest screen. Doing so will ensure that your users enjoy a seamless experience whatever size screen they are using. Google also favours mobile-friendly sites; those that don't receive a lower ranking.

8.   Concise landing pages

Remember that the primary purpose of your landing page is to convert your visitors into leads and that you have minimal time to do so. Therefore, your landing pages must get across your message as quickly and concisely as possible. Some of the crucial features of a good landing page include:

- A headline that communicates the benefits you are offering.
- A fast-loading image that illustrates that offer.
- Compelling copy that tells your story quickly.
- A form to collect visitor information.

- A clear call to action.
- No irrelevant links or navigation.

9.   Tracking your visitors

Unlike a published book, a website is not frozen in time and space. The best websites evolve along with the needs of their visitors. Some things may work from the outset; others may need extensive rework before they achieve their targets. By understanding your traffic, you can see where you need to focus your efforts and stop missing sales opportunities. Visitor tracking software makes the process easy. Here are just a few of the tracking tools to explore:

- Google Analytics – this highly featured application is free. It tracks and reports visitor information on the number and actions of visitors along with how they found you. You can set goals, track sales, and view their entire journey. It even performs real-time analytics.
- Hotjar – while Hotjar isn't free, you can try it before you buy it. It takes what you can achieve with Google Analytics to the next level. Using heatmaps, surveys and session recordings, the app provides a deep insight into how people interact with your website.
- Outfunnel – this app shines at tracking leads captured from form filling and lead scoring matrices. By focusing on leads, you can target them individually, for instance, by sending them tailored messages.

Google Analytics

Install Google Analytics into your website. Google Analytics is a free tool which helps you to understand the behaviour of your visitors. It also helps to create Goals which you can then import into Google Ads. Examples of Goals would be things like:

- Recording number of people who fill in your contact form
- Sales made
- Value of sales
- Number of downloads
- etc

To install Google Analytics simply go to https://analytics.google.com/ and sign up for free.

Google Tag Manager

Google Tag Manager (GTM for short) is an awesome tool which allows you to easily install various scripts into your website with each, for example Google Analytics, Facebook Pixels and so much more. So when installing Google Analytics, best to do it via GTM.

Visit https://tagmanager.google.com/ to learn more.

16) Step 5 - Action

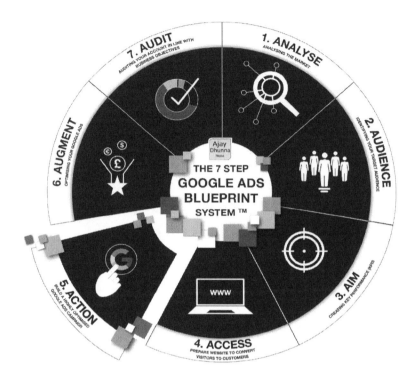

This is where we actually start building your Google Ads campaign or understanding how it is built, if you already have one.

Now remember, there are many ways you can use Google Ads to market your business, this includes:

- Google Search Ads
- Google Shopping
- Google Display Ads
- Video Ads

- Now under Discover Ads

Next, I will talk you through the fundamentals of what you need to implement and be aware of when creating your Google Ads campaigns.

For the sake of this book, I will primarily focus on Google Search Ads as these are the most common types of Ads which can be used to generate leads, enquiries, as well as great for businesses that sell online via e-commerce.

As a recap, these are the most common types of Ads on Google. Search Ads are the Text Ads that appear on the Google page when someone conducts a search. See screenshot.

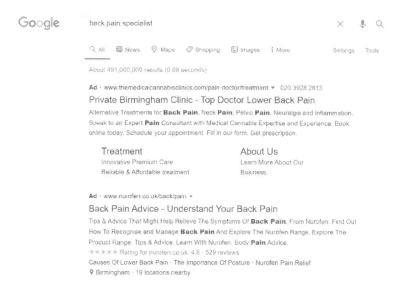

Google will show a maximum of 4 Ads at the top of the Google page and a maximum of 3 ads at the bottom of the page.

As discussed in the earlier section, your **Quality Score** will predominantly determine the amount you need to bid on a keyword in order to determine which position your Ad gets displayed at whenever someone searches for it.

Furthermore, for the purpose of this book, we will use a specific real website as a way to demonstrate what we are building a campaign for. In this case, the website (which exists at the time of writing this book is www.myhomefurniture.co.uk)

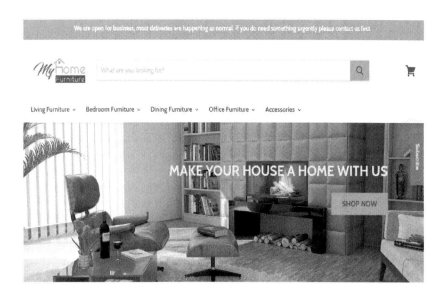

First Step – Create a "Google Account"

So, before we even start to create our Google ads account the very first thing I would recommend we do is to create an actual **Google Account**.

Creating a Google account means that any service that you use of Google you will easily be able to share data from one to another. Examples of services (as well as Google Ads) include Google Analytics, Gmail, YouTube, Google Business Profile, Google Docs and so on.

To Create a Google account simply:

1) Go to **accounts.google.com** (or your countries domain name extension i.e. Google.co.uk)
2) Select "Create an account"
3) And then select "To manage my business"

Thereafter simply follow the prompts and eventually you will end up with a new email address (i.e. <something>@gmail.com) which you can use for all the Google services.

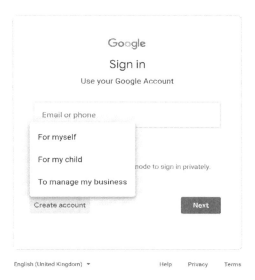

Creating Your First Google Search Ads Campaign

Now as you can see on the MyHomeFurniture.co.uk website, here there are many categories, such as Living Furniture, Bedroom Furniture etc. The more specific you are at the start the better, so rather than creating a campaign for every category let's select a specific category. In this case, let's say we are considering building a campaign for "**Office Furniture**".

You can go more specific if you like too, for example, "**office chairs**" or "**meeting chairs**" or "**Office Desks**". This really needs to be a decision which is conducted by a combination of a business decision as well as data which we have compiled from our keyword research earlier on.

124

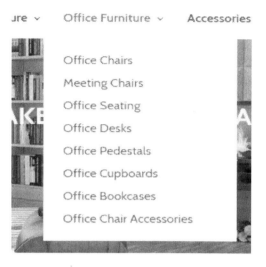

Let's say we decided we are going to market we are going to focus on **office chairs**. Thinking laterally there could be many different types of office chairs & its related accessories, so it makes sense to create a **campaign** for **office chairs**, whilst subdividing them into types of chairs, using **Ad groups**. In other words, we are catering for

1) Office Chairs
2) Meeting Chairs
3) Office Chair Accessories

Therefore the structure would look something like this...

Shortly soon, we will talk about putting our **Keywords** within each of the Ad groups.

Remember, you can always change this later, In fact, it is very rare to setup a Google Ads campaign and for it to never change. If that happens, something is not quite right!

So here are the steps we need to take:

Go to Ads.google.com

Click the "Start Now" button which will then ask if you wish to log in, or if you wish to Create an Account. Here you need to follow the prompts of basic questions related to your business in order to create a Google Ads account.

Creating your first campaign

You will then be promoted with a screen asking you, "What's your main advertising goal?" The screen will look similar to the following:

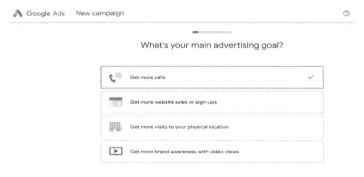

IMPORTANT: IN MY OPINION, I NEVER SELECT ANY OF THESE OPTIONS. AS BY DOING SO, YOU USUALLY GET

VERY LIMITED CONTROL AS TO WHAT YOU CAN DO WITH YOUR GOOGLE ADS CAMPAIGN, AND ARE MORE RELIANT ON GOOGLE TO MAKE MANY DECISIONS FOR YOU.

Instead, scroll down to the bottom of the page and you will see the following:

Are you a professional marketer? Switch to Expert Mode

Need help?
Call for free ad setup help at **800 169 0702**
9.00 a.m.–6.00 p.m. Mon–Fri.
More help options

Click on "**Switch to Expert Mode**"

Now this is where the real fun begins. As of now you will start creating your Google Ads campaign, and know exactly what you are doing each step of the way. The first screen you usually get prompted with is as follows:

Now remember Google changes its options and interface from time to time, so don't be alarmed if your screen looks slightly different.

I'm not going into details about these options as there is way too much to cover. Although some are self-explanatory, here's a quick summary of what each one of these are:

- **Sales** – Drive sales online, in app, by phone or in store.
- **Leads** – Get leads and other considerations by encouraging customers to take action.
- **Website Traffic** – Get the right people to visit your website.
- **Product and brand consideration** – Encourage people to explore your products or services.
- **Brand awareness and reach** – Reach a broad audience and build awareness.
- **App promotion** – Get more installs, interactions and pre-registrations for your app.
- **Local store visits and promotions** – Drive visits to local shops, including restaurants and dealerships.
- **Create a campaign without a goal's guidance** – Choose a campaign type first, without a recommendation based on your objective.
- **Create an account without a campaign** – Used commonly to help setup an account and billing, where the account can be built afterwards.

Now here's the question:

"How does selecting an option make any difference?"

The simple answer is depending on what option you select here, Google will be able to better guide you in terms of further options which be relevant to you to help you achieve your goals. So if in the event you get this wrong, don't panic, it is ok, it just means you will need to decide further options for yourself, instead of being guided by Google!

Depending on which option you select, just below this screen, you will be presented with sub-options which correspond to what you have chosen. So for example, if you select SALES, then Google Ads will say, OK, as you are looking for Sales, the campaign Type which may be suitable that may help you to achieve your objectives are:

- Search
- Display
- Discovery
- Performance Max
- Shopping
- Video

However, if on the other hand you selected BRAND AWARENESS AND REACH

- Display
- Video

For the sake of this demonstration, let's say we selected **CREATE A CAMPAIGN WITHOUT A GOAL'S GUIDANCE**. We will then be presented with all the sub options available as it is then up to us to ensure we select the appropriate campaign type.

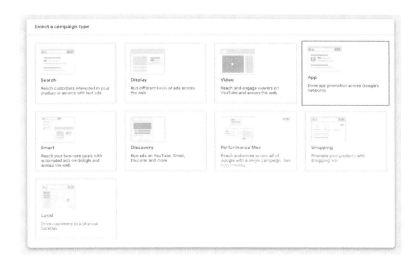

Now this is where it gets interesting. We can have multiple campaigns and multiple different types of campaigns for your products/services. For example, when selling items on an e-commerce store, we may have a Search Campaign, but we may also decide to have a Shopping campaign too. And so on.

So let's keep it simple, as ultimately this book is not about making you the best Google Ads Guru in the world but is more so to give you the ability to understand the Google Ads framework, methodology and Moreso, gaining a solid knowledge to be able to communicate at a competition level with those who may be running your Google Ads. With that being said, let's select "SEARCH", as this will allow you to create text-based ads at the top of the Google screen, whenever people look for your products and services.

Search

Reach customers interested in your product or service with text ads

Scroll down a little and Google will now ask you for some more details. This time it's asking to "**Select the results that you want to get from this campaign**". As it could be that you want to take people to your website (So that they can buy or enquires, or you may wish to receive just phone calls. Or maybe you have an App and you want people to be able to download it. You may leave everything empty if you wish. By selecting an option, it is just helping Google make more relevant recommendations to you. The screen will look somewhat like the following:

Select the results that you want to get from this campaign

☐ Website visits

☐ Phone calls

☐ App downloads

Let's select "**Website visits**". You will then be asked to type in the address of your website. i.e., **https://myhomefurniture.co.uk**

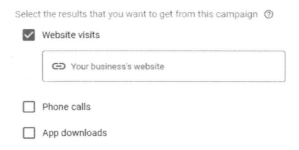

Had you selected "Phone Calls" you would have been asked to enter the phone number you want people to call you on. Likewise had you selected "App downloads" you would have been asked about the platform of your app (Android or IOS) as well as the App name.

So now let's scroll down to the last section of this page, which is "**Start tracking your website conversion**"

Ultimately, we want to be able to measure everything, from how many visits we are getting onto the website through Google Ads, how many sales (purchases) were made by people who clicked on one of our Ads, how many leads we have received and so on. What Google is asking you to do here, is to define what we wish to track and how. However, for the sake of making things easy, we will cover tracking in another section.

So for now, simply click on the CONTINUE button. This is where the fun really begins as now, we have started building our campaign. So in the next section, we will go through the settings which you can apply to the first campaign you are building.

Campaign settings

The campaign settings allow you to uniquely configure settings for each campaign you create, depending on what you wish to achieve. The campaign settings contain various sections, so let's go through each of these in turn.

General settings

- ### Campaign Name

Give each campaign a suitable name. A name which when you look at it, you know instantly what the campaign is for. The default campaign name for a search campaign is "Search-1". Never use the default names, as it is not best practice, and they are not intuitive. It is up to you to decide how you wish to format your naming convention. I usually use a combination of factors from campaign type, products or services, and location.

So, here's a suggestion of a campaign name structure you might use:

<Campaign type>-<Product or Category name>-<Location Name>

For example, I might use:

Search-Office-Chairs-London. In this way just by looking at the campaign name, I know the campaign is a **Search** campaign, I am promoting **office chairs** within the **London** area.

You can go as advanced with this as you like, but I feel the above is a good starting point. The main point I am making here is to develop a suitable and meaningful naming conversion for your campaigns.

- **Networks**

Networks tells Google, that as well as in this case, displaying your Ads on the Google page, where else might you wish to show your ads. You have 2 options:

- Include Google search partners
- Include Google Display Network

By default, both would be ticked.

Google search partners are those who have partnered with Google. These are non-Google Websites. Unfortunately, Google does not disclose who its partners are, however, if you conduct a quick search on 'search partners' you may be able to come up with a list. However, some of the most commonly known ones include YouTube, Amazon.com, as well as The New Your Times and a host of others. Tick or untick these options respectively.

[**My Top Tip**]: When starting a new campaign, we want the highest quality results, and clicks to our sites, as we are paying for each click. So for a few campaigns, I would recommend you **Untick** the "**Google Search Partners**" box so that you know that all your clicks are coming from the Google search engine page and not other websites that may have simply embedded the Google search box onto their websites.

- ## Display Network

The **Display network** allows advertisers to display an image ad or video ad on non-Google websites for example blogs, mobile apps, and some other more popular websites. You can decide if you wish this campaign to be included within the Google Display network.

Similar to search partners, you can decide whether or not you wish to allow your campaign to advertise on Googles' Display Network.

[**My Top Tip**]: Never have a search campaign and 'Display Network' targeted within the same campaign. Measuring performance and optimising such campaigns will get extremely difficult and ineffective. If you do wish to target Display Network, create a separate campaign for it so that they can be reported on, optimised, and analysed independently as their performances will vary significantly.

- ## Show more options

∨ Show more settings

The Show more option is usually a little subtle and can easily be missed. However, there are more advanced settings which you can apply. These include (which we will not go into in this book):

- Start and end dates of campaigns
- Campaign URL options (Used to help with tracking)
- Dynamic Search Ads setting
- Ad schedule (Allow you to schedule what days and times of the day you wish your ads to be shown

[**My Top Tip**]: Only if you are certain you know what days of the week, and what times of the days are you likely to get sales or enquiries, should you work on configuring scheduling options. Otherwise, leave them to serve all time towards the start of each campaign so that you allow time for sufficient data to be collected. Once collected you can then make data-driven decisions.

Targeting and Audience Segments

This section allows you to define who you wish to reach like where they are based and so on. So, let's discuss each option.

- **Locations**

The locations option allows you to specify which locations you want your ads to be displayed within. Again, start off with a small local area, build up your campaign and start expanding locations thereafter.

For example, you may wish you add to only be visible to people within London. In which case, you can specify to Google to only show your ads to people within London. By default, you have three options.

- Option 1: All countries and territories.
- Option 2: This will normally be your default country. For example, United Kingdom.
- Option 3: Enter another location.

Most of the time we would need to select the third option which says Enter another location. However, you may choose which option suits you best.

Select the third option (**Enter Another Location**) and a window will open asking you to enter a location to target or exclude. You will also see an "Advanced search" option too.

Click on **Advanced search** as you will get more options and control over the areas you wish to target as well as those areas used to exclude.

You can target people by **location name** or even by specifying a **radius** of a given **post code/zip code** or name of a city. So let's discuss location first.

Target your customers by Location

By default, the location option is selected. Start typing in the name of the location and you will see Google gives you suggestions in terms of what it thinks the location names are relevant to you.

- **Location Settings**

Try hovering your mouse over any of the locations, then on the right-hand side, you will see three options:

1) Target.
2) Exclude.
3) Nearby.

Select **target** next to the location which used to target, or you may select exclude if you wish to exclude that location. You may also select **nearby** to target the location would have specified as well as other nearby locations.

When you select **target,** you will see that the map at the right-hand side will start auto updating and highlighting the targeting areas in blue as well as the locations you have excluded in red. This helps you to give it a visual representation of your Google ads targeting. You may target or exclude as many areas as you wish.

You can also click on the "+" and "–" symbols to zoom out and in on the maps.

[**My Top Tip**]: Start off by targeting a smaller area. Get your campaigns to work and expand out gradually. This way your money works harder in those areas allowing you to scale quicker.

In the screenshot below, you can see that I have targeted London (highlighted in blue when you view in colour), and there are 2 locations which I have excluded which are shown in red).

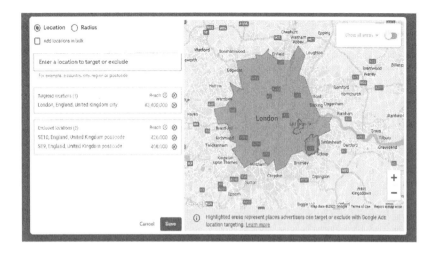

Once done, click on the **SAVE** button.

Location Options

Before we move away from Location Settings, typically of Google they hide away some of the most important options. Ironically the options they hide or recommend are the options which make them more money!

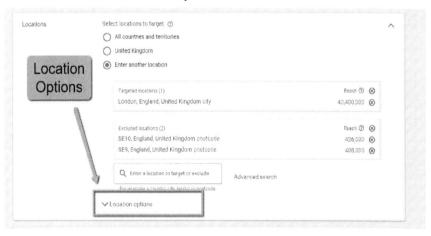

Click on **Location Options**. Here, you will be able to specify the accuracy of the targeting which you have set above. You will get a screen showing some further options:

Target ⑦

◉ Presence or interest: People in, regularly in or who've shown interest in your targeted locations (recommended)

○ Presence: People in or regularly in your targeted locations

○ Search interest: People searching for your targeted locations

Exclude ⑦

◉ Presence: People in your excluded locations (recommended)

○ Presence or interest: People in, regularly in or who've shown interest in your excluded locations

By default, the option "**Presence or interest: People in, regularly in or who've shown interest in your targeted locations (recommended)**" will be selected. This will, as the name implies, show ads to people who may not even be in your area but have shown an interest in your location.

Target

"**Presence: People in or regularly in your targeted locations**" – Here your ad will be shown to those people who are physically in your area.

"**Search interest**: People searching for your targeted locations"

[**My Top Tip**]: Consider starting your campaign with the "**Presence: People in or regularly in your targeted locations**" selected as the quality of the clicks will be much higher and relevant. This is because the audience your ads will be shown to are mostly going to be from within your local area.

Exclude

Here you can specify the accuracy of the areas you wish to Exclude.

Languages

The languages option will allow you to specify your ads to be served to people who have set their browser to a specific language as well as the language that is used on the landing page. For example, if someone has got their browser's language set to English your ads would be served to them. Likewise, if the language is set to Portuguese, you add will not be served to these people. So, it's more of a business decision that you have to use as to whether you wish to specify a language or you wish to leave the language option unspecified which means regardless of which language has been set on the browser you add would be served to those uses.

To set a language simply start typing in the name of the language. Google then also help you by showing other related options. Likewise, to take out a language, simply click on the "x" symbol next to the language you wish to take out.

[My Top Tip]: Unless your product or service specifically requires people to only speak in a certain language, consider not adding any language option at all. As with all countries, your country of residency or the country you wish to target may have people from all over the world, who may have set their browser language to their native language, all though they may be able to speak and write fluently in your local language, in my case, **English**.

Audience Segments

This is where you really need to start thinking about who your target audiences are. Look at the Avatar exercise we conducted (in section <u>Building Avatars</u>). Maybe you decided that one of the industries you wish to target is **Estate Agents**, in which case type in Estate Agency and see what options you get.

This is Super Powerful. As of now we are layering our keywords with another targeting mechanism, which is our audiences. Google can now use this information to service people who have typed in one of your keywords, AND have fallen within this audience type.

Select the audiences that you feel are relevant to you by placing a tick in the box. Your screen should look something as follows:

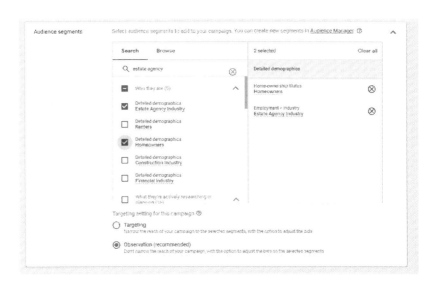

- **Targeting Google Ads with Avatars**

In the old days of Google Ads, we would target customers who searched for specific keywords, but nowadays, it has become considerably more sophisticated. We still search for people who use keywords, but we can also do far more – for instance, we can target people who share the same attributes as our avatars.

Now you have developed your avatars; you can start targeting your Google Ads. You do this by adding an audience to either your campaign or ad group. Note that Google allows you to create your own audience or choose one that has been pre-configured by Google, though as you have already developed your avatar, you will probably opt for the former, though you may wish to experiment with both. These are a selection of some of the targeting options Google offers:

- **Affinity** – provides a holistic picture of your avatar and can be used in search, display and video. This targets people who are passionate about their interests. To get a spreadsheet of affinity audiences, simple Google "**Google Ads Affinity categories**".

- **Life event** – moving home, graduating, getting married - by knowing the critical events in our avatar's life, we gain huge marketing potential.

- **In-market audiences** are people who are already researching products they are thinking of buying. Here is Google's <u>CSV</u> of the marketing segments.

- **Custom** – target audiences using keywords, website URLs, and more.

- **Custom intent** - auto-created display ads allow you to send segmented audiences to different landing pages.

- **Detailed demographics** – similar to life-event, you can find audiences that share similar traits.

- **Similar audiences** – find customers similar to existing customers through machine learning.

- ## Observation Mode

Observation settings allow you to see how a specific avatar behaves when it is an excellent match to specific criteria without limiting your ads to only showing to that target. Observation mode doesn't limit who can see your ad- it simply lets you monitor behaviour. Importantly it allows you to use custom bids to target the customer actively.

As an example of how this works, let's assume we have an online clothes shop. Sandra, your avatar, is a 22-year-old woman who is planning to get married early next year. She is very keen on keeping fit and healthy and takes exercise somewhat seriously. She is five feet six inches tall with a BMR of 23 and is interested in sporting apparel.

You have a new line of youthful-looking tennis wear you would like to promote. You don't want to restrict your audience to tennis wear, but you want to know more about your avatar. If ads for tennis wear perform differently from other ads, you can adjust your bids either higher or lower to fine-tune your campaign to that audience. You might use the additional information to create a new ad group. The fact is, with observation mode, you have much more flexibility to match your marketing to your perfect avatar.

Once you have adequate data and can see which audiences you are getting conversions from you can switch your observation to **Targeting** mode.

- **Finally**

Avatars, targeting and observation mode add extra dimensions to digital marketing. These are potent tools, so it's worth taking some time to understand them. Their only downside is that it can take some effort to really understand them and use them optimally. Any errors you might make implementing these developments could waste money and cause you to miss opportunities.

Budget and Bidding

In this section we can specify how much we wish to spend on a daily amount, as well as which bidding algorithm you would like Google Ads to use. So let's go through both of these in turn.

- **Budget**

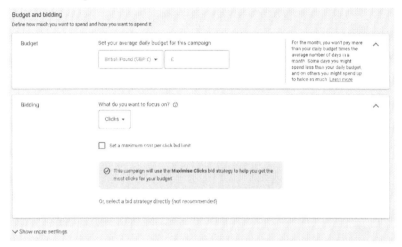

Depending on what your monthly budget is, simply divide it by 30, which will give you an estimate of your daily spend. There are more advanced ways in which you can use to set your Google Ads budget but we will not cover these here.

So if you have a monthly budget of £1,000, then your daily budget will need to be set to ~£33. Type this amount into the box which shows your currency symbol. If you wish to setup multiple campaigns, then you need to divide this budget amongst your campaigns.

Ensure you have the correct currency set from the list box option.

Also note, whatever budget you have specified, if it is not spent, Google will not try to force the spend. It will remain as unspent and will be reset the following day.

A word of caution: Google reserves the right to spend up to twice your daily budget on specific days where Google deems it is more likely to drive conversions, although it will ensure the average amount you spend during the month, remains as whatever you had specified it to be.

[My Top Tip]: Start off on a small budget, but ensure it is big enough to start attracting a reasonable number of clicks and conversions quickly. In this way, you will spend less time worrying about what works and what does not and will be able to make fast decisions on the optimisations you need to carry out in order to allow the account to start getting your campaign to perform well.

- **Bidding**

Bidding in Google Ads allows you to tell Google, what type of algorithm you want Google to use to help you achieve your objectives when deciding how much it needs to bid, to get a click on a given keyword.

There are various bidding strategies you can use with Google. Each campaign can have its own bidding strategy. Next, we will go through the most popular bidding strategies, to give you an idea of what each one does.

You will be asked to select which you wish to focus on. Unsurprisingly, the default will be 'Clicks' (We know Google makes a shedload of money from Clicks, whether they convert into sales for you or not!)

In order to use the cleverer bidding strategies, you must have conversion tracking installed, although you should have this installed regardless of which strategies you wish to use.

When you click on the option **Clicks** from the list box, you will see some options. To reveal all the options, you may need to click on **Other optimisation options**. Your screens should look something as follows:

So, in summary, here are some of the popular bidding options:

Clicks

This tells Google, that you wish to get as many clicks as possible, within your given budget. There are very few reasons why anyone would want to use this. However, some reasons may include:

- When an account or campaign has been newly setup, and you wish to get some data, use optimise a campaign. Once you have enough data, and ideally conversions, you could consider changing this bid strategy to one of the smarter bid strategies listed below.

- Brand campaigns, so you may wish your ads to come up as much as possible when anyone types in any of your brand keywords.

Impression share

Impression share allows you to tell Google, to adjust your bid, according to where you would like your Ad to appear on the Google page. Options available are:

- **Anywhere on the results page.**
- **Top of results page.** In this case, your ad may appear anywhere within the top 4 Ad slots of the google results page. Remember there are also 3 ad slots available at the bottom of the page too.
- **Absolute top of results page.** With this strategy, you are telling Google you would like your ad to appear at the very top of the 4 ad slots available on the google results page.

Regardless of which option you have chosen above, you will get two further options.

1) **Percentage (%) impression share to target.** This allows you to specify what percentage of the tie you wish Google to use the bidding strategy you have selected.

2) **Maximum CPC bid limit**. Here you can specify to Google that it can bid as much as it likes, as long as it does not exceed a specific Cost-per-click.

My Top Tip: Always specify a Maximum CPC bid limit otherwise, you are allowing Google to bid as much as it wants for a specific keyword, which could easily burn your budget very quickly.

Maximise conversions

This is by far one of my favourite bidding strategies. Here you can specify to Google that you want the Google algorithm to bring you as many conversions as possible. This could be people filling in contact forms, appointment forms, booking valuations, or clicking on links to call or email you.

Only use this option if
    a)   You have a conversion tracking setup.
    b)   You have at least 15 conversions within the last 30-day window. This will mean google has got some data to base its decisions on.

Additionally, you can specify a Target Cost Per Action (Target CPA) (This option is only available once you have adequate data). For example, it could be that you sell a product for £500 and make £200 profit from each one. So, you could even specify that I want a maximum target CPA to be let's say £100. i.e. for every £100 you spend, you want to win one sale!

[My Top Tip]: You can setup multiple conversion actions, for example, track purchases as well as how many people filled in a form. This allows you to tightly manage what you consider a conversion.

Maximise Conversion Value

This is different to the **Maximise Conversions** bid strategy in that in this case we are telling Google we wish to get as much **revenue** as possible. Google will then use its algorithm to determine how it needs to conduct its bidding.

It is not as simple as the most expensive products get the highest bid. As it could be that a lower priced product sells more and will therefore generate more revenue. Google will therefore favour that one a product which may be more expensive but will not generate much revenue.

To use Maximise conversion value bid strategy, it is essential that you have revenue data tracked alongside your conversions.

Again, with Maximise Conversion Value, you also have the ability to specify what target Return On Ad Spend (ROAS) you wish to aim for i.e. 500%!

Manual CPC

With Manual CPC (Manual Cost-Per-Click), it is a non-automated, non-smart bid strategy, You decide exactly what you wish to pay per click, per keyword, manually. Although this gives you a lot of control, you should only use this as an advanced user as Google's algorithm will not help you to adjust bids, based on who is more likely to convert or not.

I usually use Manual CPC bid strategies at the start of a campaign whilst I am assessing the performance of a campaign, or whilst conducting experiments.

There is however a small sub option available called "**Enhanced CPC**" which you can optionally tick. I personally have never found this to work well. This is Google's way or saying, allow us to get more conversions from your manual

CPC bidding, by raising CPC bids for clicks that are more likely convert into a lead or sale.

So for now, let's select **Maximise Clicks** bid strategy.

Setting up the ad groups

Now, a quick recap, The Ad groups is where we have logically broken down the campaign into its own themes. In this way, we can make sure the Ads that people see when they search for the products or services are very relevant and specific to the corresponding keywords. Refer to diagram below:

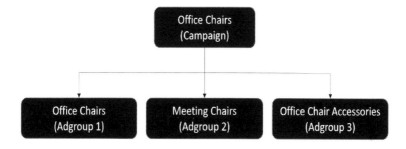

Here you can see we plan on creating 3 Ad groups, in the campaign "Office Chairs":

1) **Office Chairs** (Although this is the same name as the main campaign, this ad group will contain keywords specifically if people search keywords relating to only 'Office chairs'.

2) **Meeting Chairs** – Here we can make sure all the keywords in this ad group are related to meeting

chairs only. Consequently, the Ads we create, we can make sur they are all related to Meeting room chairs specifically. Examples of keywords we might use here may be:

    a.   Leather meeting chairs

    b.   Meeting chairs with wheels

    c.   Etc.

3) **Office Chair Accessories** – In this ad group, as with meeting chairs, we can ensure all keywords are related to "office chair accessories"!

The way we build the ad groups is you do not need to build them out all in one-go. Build just the first one, finish the first complete setup of the campaign, then come back and start adding more ad groups as you wish.

-    **Ad group type**

By default, the first option you get is Standard. This is the one we will use. However, if you click the listbox the other option you get is "Dynamic". This is a little more advanced in that Google will use the text on your website and will automatically create headlines which it feels are relevant. So, for now, let's just move onto the next section.

• Ad group Name

Ad group name

> Ad group 1

This is where we give the name for our Ad group. The name Google gives you by default will be "Ad group 1". Never use the default names. Always use a meaningful naming convention. So, in this case, let's start with creating an ad group for "meeting chairs". So, let's delete the default name and type in, you got it, "**Meeting Chairs**".

• Keywords

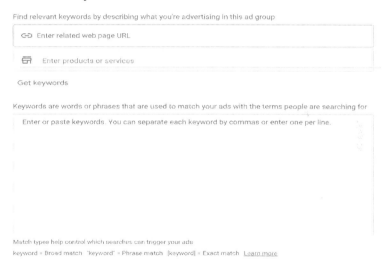

Find relevant keywords by describing what you're advertising in this ad group

⊖ Enter related web page URL.

🖥 Enter products or services

Get keywords

Keywords are words or phrases that are used to match your ads with the terms people are searching for

Enter or paste keywords. You can separate each keyword by commas or enter one per line.

Match types help control which searches can trigger your ads
keyword = Broad match   "keyword" = Phrase match   [keyword] = Exact match   Learn more

The first 2 sections here are there to help Google automatically suggest keywords for you. For example, you may type your website URL and click on "Get keywords". Google will then go to that URL and put a whole load of keywords into the

"Enter or paste keywords" box. Likewise, you can type in the name of a product or service and again hit "Get keywords". Again, google will suggest keywords for you.

Although you may find this attractive, I tend to stay clear of this as I find most of the keywords Google suggest are not of great quality in terms of their relevance, or "intent to buy". So I prefer to research and type my own keywords.

[**My Top Tip**]: If you do get Google to get your keywords for you, just ensure you go through them very carefully and take out those you feel are not suitable, else you could end up spending a whole load of money on poor quality keywords.

Keywords are words or phrases that are used to match your ads with the terms people are searching for.

Now this is the section you actually enter your keywords into.

We will cover researching keywords like a pro in the Augment section. For now, we just need to make sure we have a few of the obvious and basic keywords ready.

So have a careful think, using what you have learned about keyword intent in the Categorising Keywords section. So for now, let's use keywords which we feel people would only be searching these if they have an intent to buy. You must pit each keyword in a new line. I suggest adding around 3-5 keywords to start with. As later on, once you have researched these keywords further you may like to go in and edit them.

Or if you have already researched them, just feel free to type them in now. Let's use the following keywords:

- blue stackable chairs
- cost of meeting room chairs
- wooden meeting room chairs

Note: In Google Ads, the keywords you specify and not case-sensitive, although I like and prefer to use lower-case for consistency and my form of best practices.

This is where the fun begins. Not only do we have keywords we also have keyword "**Match Types**".

What are Match Types?

Match Types is additional information we provide to Google, which allows Google to determine how closely the keyword you have specified, needs to match with whatever the user has typed in (or more technically the users search query). To do this, we need to understand 4 match types Google supports (There was a 5th, but Google has recently depleted it. It was called Broad Match Modifiers – But I'll explain what it did anyway.) These are:

1. Broad Match
2. Broad Match Modifiers (depleted as of July 2021)
3. Phrase Match
4. Exact Match
5. Negative Match

So, let's discuss these one by one to give you a summary of what each one is, and how it works.

- **Broad Match**

Broad Match keywords allow your ad to be shown for the widest range of keyword searches, that are related to a keyword you have specified. Now let's put that into simpler English. Your Ad can be shown, as long as all the keywords are part of the search, regardless of word order. However, close variations of the keywords and synonyms may are allowed.

Isn't it funny how Broad Match is the default and is where Google will make most of its income from?

Examples of broad match keywords

Keyword	Symbol	Format you would use in Google Ads	Your Ad may be triggered for these keywords
tennis shoes	None	tennis shoes	<ul><li>mens tennis shoes</li><li>tennis trainers</li><li>tennis running shoes</li><li>socks for running</li><li>Boys tennis boots</li></ul>

One major advantage of using broad match is it allows you to discover new keywords that you could utilise within your Google Ads campaign, for keywords you may not had considered. On the downside, you could end up getting clicks for a lot of irrelevant or low-quality searches, so you really need to be very consistent when analysing your search terms and negative keyword.

- **Broad Batch Modifiers**

As stated earlier, Broad Match Modifier was depleted in July 2021. My reason for including this here is it shocks me to see how many Google Ads campaigns are still using this and have not yet made changes to their accounts. You really need to be replacing these with a broad match or phrase match.

Broad match modifiers are where you can specify a number of keywords, preceded with a plus symbol (+). This is then telling Google Ads, that your Ad may be triggered, as long as all the keywords which you have specified, are contained within whatever a user has typed in. Your ad will be triggered regardless of the order in which the keywords appear, as well as whether there are additional keywords which the user has typed in. Google will also trigger your ad for close variations

Personally, I use to absolutely love this match type and was pretty gutted when Google decided to scrap it.

Examples of broad match modifier keywords

Keyword	Symbol(s)	Format you would use in Google Ads	Your Ad may be triggered for these keywords
tennis shoes	+	+tennis +shoes	• mens tennis shoes • tennis running shoes • how much are red tennis shoes

The main advantage is broad match modifiers was it gave you greater control to ensure the keywords you have specified, will be part of what the user has typed in, but in addition, you may discover other combinations of keywords that you can either use or make into negatives if they are not relevant to you.

- **Phrase Match**

With phrase match, you need to put your keywords within double quotes. Google will then only trigger your ad if a user has typed in your keywords, in the same order that you specified. Once again, Google will allow for close variations.

Examples of phrase match keywords

Keyword	Symbol(s)	Format you would use in Google Ads	Your Ad may be triggered for these keywords
tennis shoes	" "	"tennis shoes"	• mens tennis shoes • tennis shoes • how much are red tennis shoes

The advantage of phrase match is you get much greater control as your ad will only appear if users have typed in your keywords in the order you specified, but with the additional benefit of allowing keywords to be specified both before and after too.

Due to the increased quality, it also, therefore, helps you to better manage your budget as you know your average cost-per-click will go towards keywords that are more relevant to your business, thus avoiding too much wasted spend.

Phrase match is becoming my favourite match type as it has tight control over the keywords and phrases you use but allows you to see what additional search terms your phrase match might trigger. You can then decide if it is relevant, or if you need to add it in as a negative keyword.

- **Exact Match keywords**

Exact match is exactly that. Google will attempt to show your ads when a user types in exactly what you have specified. However, lately, Google has amended its algorithm to make 'exact match' to 'not so much exact match' which is very annoying. What I mean by this is Google will firstly allow close variations, and secondly, it will allow your ad to be triggered for keywords which Google deems to have the same intent or meaning, as what you have specified! Having said that, using exact match is the closest you will get to triggering your ads for only keywords which you have specified. The keyword a user types in must be in the same order, as well as not having any leading or trailing keywords too.

Examples of exact match keywords

Keyword	Symbol(s)	Format you would use in Google Ads	Your Ad may be triggered for these keywords
tennis shoes	[ ]	[tennis shoes]	• tennis shoes • tennis shoe • tennis trainers

Apart from now having to keep a closer eye on the search terms which trigger your ads, and ensuring you implement negative keywords where necessary, exact match will be the highest quality keywords to trigger your ads and will give you the greatest control over the cost per clicks.

Negative Keywords

A common mistake I find when we take on accounts within our agency, is people pay a lot of attention to the keywords they wish to include and have their ads shown for, but very little emphasis on the keywords they wish to avoid their ads being shown for. It is equally important, if not more, to tell Google which keywords you do not want your ads to be shown for. This is called 'Negative Keywords".

Considering what you have learnt in the keyword match types section you can see your ad may be triggered for a product or service you do not cater for. Or even, your ad may be triggered for keywords where people are only researching and have no intent to buy. We then need to add these keywords as Negative Keywords.

Negative keywords can be added at Campaign Level, or Ad Group level. Campaign level means you can avoid any searches that contain your negative keyword within that campaign, and if specified at ad group level, the negative keyword will only apply to that specific ad group.

It is therefore imperative you keep a regular check on the search terms that trigger your ads to be shown for, and add them in as negative keyword if need be.

So, let's continue building out the ad group

By now your keyword section should look something as follows.

Find relevant keywords by describing what you're advertising in this ad group

GⱭ Enter related web page URL

⌂ Enter products or services

Update keywords

Keywords are words or phrases that are used to match your ads with the terms people are searching for

blue stackable chairs
cost of meeting room chairs
wooden meeting room chairs

Match types help control which searches can trigger your ads
keyword = Broad match "keyword" = Phrase match [keyword] = Exact match Learn more

However, taking into account what we have learnt about match types you may decide to add more keywords into it. Note: You may have a mixture of match types within an ad group, although we will not discuss this within this book, as I feel they are more along the lines of implementing advanced strategies. Consequently, it could therefore be your keywords box looks along the following lines:

Keywords are words or phrases that are used to match your ads with the terms people are searching for

blue stackable chairs
cost of meeting room chairs
wooden meeting room chairs
[office meeting chairs]
"office chairs"

Match types help control which searches can trigger your ads
keyword = Broad match "keyword" = Phrase match [keyword] = Exact match Learn more

At this stage, we can go on to create more Ad groups, although I would advise against it. I would suggest you finish off building your complete Google Ads account, and then going back and building the account out.

So now let's click on the "**Save and Continue**" button.

Setting up your Ads

Your Ads is the first thing people will see on the Google page, which will ultimately determine whether they click on it to visit your website, or your competitors.

It is therefore crucial to ensure you send out the correct message which accurately promotes your products or services.

Having well thought-out ads, which accurately describe your products and services, means you are likely to attract the right audience, who are actively looking for your products or services. Similarly, having poorly designed Ads may lead to a large number of people clicking on the ads, but achieving very few sales or leads, which will ultimately lead to an unnecessary increase in costs.

On a final point, before we go into writing your ads, it is important to understand that not only are we trying to attract people to click on our ads, but we equally wish to disqualify people who may not be the right audience for us. What I mean by that is, let's say the products you sell have a starting price of £500. By mentioning this in the ad copy, i.e., "Prices start from £500", those people who may have only had a budget of £100, are now less likely to click on your ad. As a result, you have not had to pay Google for a click, which would never have converted.

Your screen will look something as follows when you first go into it to setup your ads.

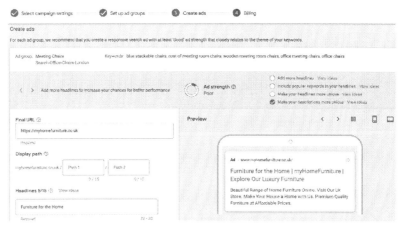

Let's start from the top and work our way down. This screen will allow you to design an Ad. Technically the ad is known as a "Responsive Search Ad" (or RSAs).

Responsive Search Ads in Google are replacing the traditional "Expanded Text Ads" (or ETA ads).

ETA allowed you to specify exactly what text you wanted to show on the Google page and Google will display just those headlines and descriptions which you have specified. ETA ads had 3 Headlines and 2 Description lines. However, these are being depleted starting June 2022.

RSAs however allow you to specify up to 15 Headlines and 4 Description lines. Based on what the user has searched for, Google will determine which is the best combination of headlines and descriptions to show to the user on the Google page.

So now let's jump onto each of the main sections of the ad creation page.

- **Ad Strength**

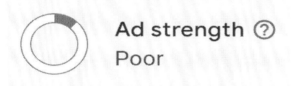

The Ad strength is an important indicator as to how well Google thinks your ads have been written. It goes from:
- Poor
- Average
- Good
- Excellent

Needless to say, you need to aim for Excellent, but anything between **Good** and **Excellent**, is Excellent 😊

Google's definition of Ad Strength is:

"Ad strength is an indication of the relevance and diversity of your ad combinations. Having more relevant and unique content can help you get the right ad in front of your customers and improve your ad's performance."

As and when you fill in your headlines and description lines, the ad strength should change.

On the right-hand side of the page, you will find a section where Google attempts to help and guide you as to what you should do, to increase your ad strength. Be sure to click on "view ideas" to help you wish this.

Essentially Google is looking for a variety of headlines and descriptions, which are different, but highly relevant. So, try to add a combination of headlines to include:

- Headlines which say what your product is (ensure to include your main keywords)
- Your Unique Selling Points (USPs)
- Any Offers, discounts (Such as Unbeatable Prices, Price Match Guarantee)
- Call-To-Actions (Such as Order Online, Book Now)
- Trust Phrases (Such as Official Website, 5 x Rated, 30 Day Refund Guarantee)

○ Add more headlines   View ideas
○ Include popular keywords in your headlines   View ideas
○ Make your headlines more unique   View ideas
✓ Make your descriptions more unique   View ideas

- ## **Preview**

On the right-hand side of the page, you will see a preview. This is updated continuously to show you how your ad may look like on the Google page. You will see it has a Mobile icon and Desktop icon too. Click on these to see how your ad may look like on each of these devices.

- ## **Final URL**

Enter the landing page you would like your users taken to, who click on your Ad. Remember your home page is not necessarily a good page to take people to. Ensure the page people get taken to is the most relevant page according to what they may have searched for.

- **Display Path**

Google allow you to specify 2 path names, which Google will show as part of your Ad text. This is an opportunity for you to specify some highly relevant keywords. What you type here will not affect what page your users end up on, as that's determined in the Final URL field, so these are more vanity fields to aid click-though. So, in this case, I may enter "meeting-room" in Path 1, and "Chairs" in Path 2.

- ## Headlines

Furniture for the Home

Required   22 / 30

Delivery available

Required   18 / 30

myHomeFurniture

Required   15 / 30

Make Your House A Home

22 / 30

Explore Our Luxury Furniture

28 / 30

New headline

0 / 30

You may enter up to 15 headlines, each one must be a maximum of 30 characters. Once again, click on "View Ideas" for inspiration as to what you could type in as Google may make recommendations. And remember to vary the headlines, so that you can allow Google to make better decisions as to which headline it should display to the user. I would recommend a minimum of 5 headlines, although the more the better.

- ## Descriptions

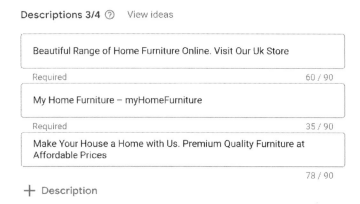

You may enter up to 4 description lines, each one being up to 9 characters each. Once again, use a variety of different headlines and keep an eye on the Ad Strength.

Once done, hit the "Done" button and click Save and Continue button.

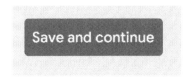

What makes a Good Ad Copy?

To have a good Ad Copy, in other words, the text you use in your Ads, it is good to use a combination of **types** of headlines and **types** descriptions which consist of some or more of the following:

Call To Action phrases. What would you like people to do when they read your Ad? For example, "Call Now", "Get A Quote", "Get In Touch", "Learn More".

Your main Keyword. Ensure to include your main keyword or phrase within your headlines & descriptions.

Unique Selling Points. What are your USPs which make you stand out from your competitors? Ensure to include these. For example, "Same Day Service", "Next Day Delivery", etc.

Promotions/Special Offers. Are there any promotions or special offers you can include to entice your readers to click on your Ads? For example, "50% Off", "Buy One Get One Free".

Trust-related phrases. Include phrases which may help people to build trust with you, for example, "5 X rating", "Family Business", and "Official Website".

Phrases which address your audience's pain points. This is where we tap into what problems they may be facing. For example, "Bills too high?" "Not getting enough sales"? Essentially it is a pain point your customer may be able to relate to.

Sense of urgency. You want your customers to act now, right? So why must they act fast? Include phrases such as "Sale Ends Today", "Only 24 Items Remaining", and "Limited Availability".

Location Phrases. It also helps to include your geographical locations, as people will be comforted that you provide your service within that location.

Conclusion for writing professional Ad Copy

When coming up with strong headline ideas, it's worth thinking about what benefits your product or service delivers to the audience.

Benefits are future-focused and revolve around what the outcome is. For example, if you are a lawn services firm, you may offer a grass cutting service. That is a feature. What your audience want is a benefit: to be able to look at their beautiful lawn, or let their children play on the lawn or sit out in their garden when the weather is good. Crucially, each of these benefits has emotion attached to it.

The reason why this is important is that by bringing an emotional element into your headlines, it will connect with the reader in a different from other ads they may be reading.

A page of Google search results can look very confusing to a reader who is trying to navigate lots of different options. It can be very hard to choose between search results, both ads and organic.

However, by bringing more benefit and emotion-led language into your ad copy, it is possible to stand out on the page. If you reader feels understood, they will feel greater trust and belief that you can deliver.

For example, if you were an accountancy firm and you wanted alternative headlines and ad copy to look enticing to your potential customer, it pays to speak to how they are thinking.

If they're looking for an accountancy firm on Google, it's probably because they need their taxes done. And most people who need their taxes done, need them done quickly.

So instead of:

Tax compliance service (which is descriptive and technically explains what you do.

You can say:

Get your return done this week (which is what the reader actually wants).

This approach brings in benefits, urgency and speaks directly to the pain they are feeling.

Figure out what do they want right now. The more you speak to that need in your ad copy, the more likely they are to click.

Confirm Payment Info

We now come onto the final, and last part of officially having setup the first campaign, although we do need to go back and expand on it.

This is where we add the billing details.

Here you simply need to read all the prompts and add your billing details into it.

A word of caution Ensure you get your "Billing Country" and "Time zone" correct, as this cannot be changed at a later date.

If you have a promotional code, you may click on the pencil icon and enter it here.

Depending on which country you are in, the method of payment may vary. However, the standard is:
- Add Credit or Debit Card
- PayPal
- Direct Debit

Once you have entered your billing details, simply click on the Submit button.

Google may take up to 3 working days to approve your billing details, although it is usually a lot sooner.

Once done, you will be presented with a Congratulation screen and can then click Explore Campaigns to move onto the next step.

Refining your Google Ads campaign

Now that you have built your first campaign, this is not where it stops. You need to go back and refine the campaign, to ensure it is well built, and is built for success and profitability from day-one! Remember, we built the first campaign so that we can go through the full cycle of setting up the campaign, building a basic campaign then entering the billing details.

So here are the things you need to do to build your campaign out.

There are several parts of the Google Ads account you will want to refine. These are:

- Ad Extensions
- Campaigns
- Ad groups
- Keywords
- Ads

Refining Ad Extensions

Ad extensions allow you to attach more business-related information on your ads, as well as providing your potential customer with more information, as the ads are then naturally bigger, they attract a higher clickthrough rate too!

It is therefore crucial you take your time on adding in as many relevant Ad extensions as possible. Whilst doing so, ensure you have carefully filled all fields such as:

- Landing page
- Optional Descriptions
- Images where required

[My Top Tip]: Take a look at what extensions your competitors might be using. Be careful not to click on their ads as it's not right for you to incur them costs unnecessarily. Once you have researched these, the idea is not to copy them, but model what you like and improve upon it.

Extensions can be added at various levels including:

- Account level
- Campaign level
- Ad group level

The main ones which will discuss here are as follows:

- Sitelink Extensions
- Call Extensions
- Callout Extensions
- Location Extensions

Sitelink Extensions

Sitelinks are the most common extensions used within Google Ads. Sitelink extensions allow you to add additional links onto your ad. The links would be to other pages of your website, which you may consider relevant to the campaign you are creating.

Look at this example below:

Ad · https://www.cityosteopathsmanchester.co.uk/ ▾ 0161 839 6611
Massage - Chiropractor
City Osteopaths is an independent osteopathic practice based in Manchester city centre. Osteopath clinic in running in Manchester City Centre since 2004. Diagnosis for back pain.

prices
Concession prices Treatment price

contact us
Email us Osteopath inquiry

This Ad uses two sitelink extensions. "**Prices**" and "**Contact us**". As you can see the amount of space the Ad takes up is now much bigger. It also gives people the opportunity to go to other relevant parts of your website.

To add a site link extension,

1) Click on the campaign or ad group you would like to add it in for (or you can click on All Campaigns then Overview) if you would like it to be at account level, meaning all campaigns will use it)

2) Click Ads & Extensions

3) Click Extensions. You will be taken to a screen similar to the one below

4) Here you can either click on the link "Sitelink" or click the blue button and select Sitelink. Thereafter, you will need to fill in the site links you would like added

My recommendations for site links are:
1) Have at least 6 sitelinks
2) Try to really think, for people who are looking for your products and services, what might they feel is very relevant to them (i.e., Contact us, size guide, other relevant product categories, about us, etc). In the case of the furniture shop, sitelinks might be:
   a. Contact us
   b. Request a quote
   c. Office Tables
   d. Office Accessories
   e. Size guide
3) When adding sitelink, ensure you also type in a description, in the description field, which describes what the link is, and maybe how it may benefit them

Call Extensions

Many businesses win more customers when people call them, instead of filling in a form on your website. Consequently, such companies would much rather prefer their potential to call them via phone. As such, these companies can use the 'Call Extension'.

When you use a call extension, your phone number will appear on the Google page, as a clickable link. So, for those people who are using mobile phones to search, a user can simply click on your phone number, which will in turn call a pre-specified number. This is great as you have now generated a lead, without the user even visiting your website!

To implement a call extension:

1) Click on the campaign or ad group you would like to add it in for (or you can click on All Campaigns then Overview) if you would like it to be at account level, meaning all campaigns will use it)

2) Click Ads & Extensions

3) Click on Call Extension

You will see a subtle link called "Advanced option". Once again, Google has a habit of hiding the options which will save you money, but coincidentally, will make them more!

Most businesses are not open 24 hours, 7 days a week. By clicking on advanced options, bit only can you select which device you prefer to show your phone number on, but more importantly, which days of the week you would like it displayed, as well as what times of the day. There is little point in advertising your phone number during out of hours workday and time.

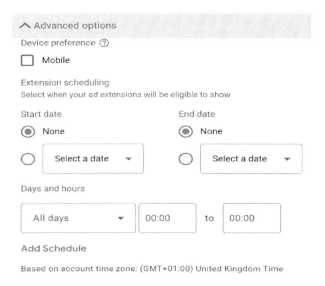

Callout Extensions

Firstly, avoid making the mistake of confusing **call extensions** with **callout extensions**. They are very different. Callout extensions are used to highlight some of your main selling points, These are displayed as non-clickable links. So, examples where you might use these are to emphasise things like:

- Delivery timescales i.e. Next Day Delivery
- Guarantee (i.e., 30 days Guarantee)
- Free Consultation

To implement a callout extension:

1) Click on the campaign or ad group you would like to add it in for (or you can click on All Campaigns then Overview) if you would like it to be at account level, meaning all campaigns will use it)
2) Click Ads & Extensions
3) Click on Callout Extension

Location Extensions

Location extensions are a must for businesses who provide local services. You need to firstly have an account on **Google Business Profile** which you can do by visiting **business.google.com**. You can then connect this to your Google Ads account. Then using Location extensions, you can promote your Google Business Profile, as well as company address, phone number and map marker.

To implement a Location extension:

1) Click on the campaign or ad group you would like to add it in for (or you can click on All Campaigns then

Overview) if you would like it to be at account level, meaning all campaigns will use it)

2) Click Ads & Extensions
3) Click on Location Extension

There you will find several options to help you set these up,

Refining Campaigns

See what other campaigns you might like to build, which will support the budget you have to work with, as well as business your requirements/priorities.

It could be that for example, if you are selling meeting chairs, you might like to setup a campaign for complimentary products such as office tables, or office accessories, and so on.

Having different campaigns also allows you to better manage your budgets as you can focus your budgets over your priority campaigns. It also allows you to specify different targeting, bid strategies and so much more.

Whilst on the topic of campaigns, not only would you want to think which campaigns you can build for your products or services, but also what types of campaigns. Remember, Google allows you to build campaigns for many platforms such as:

- Display Campaigns
- Video campaigns
- Discovery Campaigns

- …and so much more

By doing so, you are potentially tapping into new audiences to help promote your products and services.

Refining Ad Groups & Keywords

I have intentionally put these into 1 title, as they work very much hand-in-hand.

Review what other related products or services you might need, including variations of the products. For example, within the campaign we discussed earlier, (**Search-Office-Chairs-London**), we had you an Ad group which we had created called "**meeting chairs**".

Now, you might say, well, it's great having a generic Meeting Chairs Ad group, but maybe you also want to have some more specific ones too. In that way, the "ads" you create for them, can be more tailored respectively. For example, how about creating the following new Ad groups:

- Office meeting chairs
- Wooden meeting room chairs
- Leather meeting room chairs
- Upholstery meeting room chairs
- … I think you get the drift by now

Now let's say you wish to create an Ad group for **leather meeting room chairs**, what this means is that:

a) All the keywords within that Ad group can be around the word 'leather' (for example, leather meeting room chairs, leather office chairs, swivel leather meeting room chairs etc.

b) The Ads you create for this Ad group are now much more focused, towards leather meeting room chairs.

Here's something useful to know. If you already have an Ad group and wish to create a similar Ad group, rather than creating it from scratch, you can simply copy and paste one that you already have by:

1) Placing a tick in the Ad group you wish to copy
2) Click 'Edit'
3) Click 'Paste'

In this way, you have almost cloned the Ad group, including the keywords and Ads, now all you need to do is to amend the keywords, Ad group name and Ads that belong to it.

[My Top Tip]: As we wish to push all the traffic/visitors who are looking for leather meeting room chairs to this Ad group, it may be worth considering making 'leather meeting room chairs' into a Negative keyword within the genetic 'meeting room chairs' Ad group. In that way, this Ad group is now likely to attract all the traffic for these keywords, instead of some of it going to other Ad groups.

Refining Keywords

When we created the campaign, we added our initial set of keywords to help us get started. In the previous section, we also discussed adding more Ad groups and adding keywords into them. Now might be a good time to expand further and review the keywords we have in our existing Ad groups. This is the time to use your Keyword research exercise we discussed in the <u>Keyword Research Like a pro</u> section, where I also suggested downloading my free keyword research template.

This is also known as keyword expansion. The process of looking at your keywords to see what other combinations of keywords we might like to add. Whilst at it, always having at the back of your mind the 3 categories of keywords we discussed. As a reminder, these would be:

- Research intent keywords
- Buying intent keywords
- Negative keywords

…with the additional consideration of 'Match types'.

To Add Keywords, you simply go into your Campaign, then Ad group, and click on the Blue "+" icon.

You will notice a box opens where you can add your keywords into it.

Based on your existing keywords, Google will now also give you suggestions as to which other keywords you can add. The section will look similar to the following:

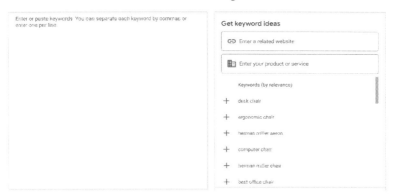

You can choose to simply click the "+" symbol next to any keyword you add. Please note that when Google adds these keywords into your keyword box, the default match type is 'Broad Match'. It is then up to you to decide if you wish to keep it as broad match, or you wish to change it to another match type such as Phrase Match or Exact Match.

[**My Top Tip**]: You can make keywords which you have added into your keyword box, into a Negative keyword, by simply placing a Minus sign next to a keyword. So, for example, if you do not want your ads to show if someone types the word 'Blue' you can simply add in:

-blue

This will then add the word blue, as a negative keyword, into that Ad group

You may also get keyword ideas by typing your website address into the "**Enter a related website**", or you can type something into the "**Enter your product or service**" box.

Refining Your Ads

Your Ads, as a reminder, is what your customers will see when they search for products or services on Google. Having a well written Ad could mean driving high quality traffic to your website. A poorly written ad could result in losing potential clicks, as well as encouraging clicks from people who are not likely to materialise onto a conversion, whether that be a lead or sale. It is therefore crucial that you spend time crafting your Ads, not just to attract potential customers, but also to deter some audiences not to click on your ad.

At the time of writing this book, we have 2 main types of Ads:
- Expanded Text Ads
- Responsive Search Ads

Expanded Search Ads are soon being phased out starting 30 June 2022, where you will no longer be able to create new Expanded Text Ads, although you may continue to use the ones you already have. It will only be matter of time before Google completely takes away Expanded Text Ads.

For now, ensure you have related 3 Ads in each Ad group, whereas at least one of the Ads is a Responsive Search Ad. At the same time ensure all ads are related to the Ad group they belong to. Vary the Ads, to ensure you use different types of

Headlines & Descriptions, as this is the only real way to see which Ads are working and those that are not.

Last but not least, ensure the Ad Strength of each ad is at least "Good", as discussed earlier.

Refining Your Budget

Check your budget. Google allows you to set your budget at campaign level. So, each campaign can have their own budget. As a result, you have total control of how much Google can spend on any specific campaign.

However, Google also allows you to have a "Shared budget". This is where you can specify an amount, let's say £100 per day, and tell Google, which campaigns are allowed to share this budget. To do this, firstly setup your shared budget by clicking on:

- Tools and Settings
- Shared Budget

From here you simply:

1) Give the budget a name, for example, "Chairs budget".
2) Select which campaigns you want the budget to be shared amongst. In the screenshot below, as we only have 1 campaign, we can only assign it to that campaign, otherwise you can select as many campaigns as you like.
3) Finally, specify the amount you wish to allocate per day amongst the chosen campaign.

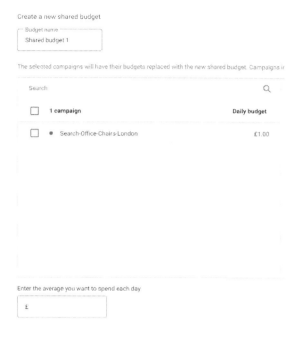

Why use a shared budget? Sometimes you might find you have created several very related campaigns for a particular product or service and have a specific budget you can allocate to that product or service. So, to avoid unnecessary granular calculations, it is sometimes easier just to use a shared budget instead which could make management a whole lot easier. Or even sometimes you may wish to test campaigns out when they are first created but have limited budget. So again, this can help in the short-term whilst you are getting to know the campaigns.

Next Steps After Refining?

So now you have built a campaign (or a few) and you want to know what you can do immediately. As harsh as it may sound, the answer is nothing. Well, at least for 2 to 3 days, depending on the size and complexity of the campaign. Don't panic. Rome wasn't built overnight.

Leave it alone for a few days, as in the next section, I will show you exactly what you need to do to ensure your campaign(s) are built for success, right from the start!

Jump onto the next section and let me go through this with you.

17) Step 6 - Augment

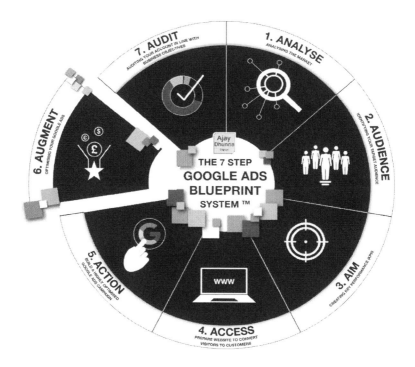

In previous chapters, I showed you how to research, create & launch Google Ads campaigns. That is really just the start.

In this section, I show you how you can enhance your campaign for success. We call this the Augment stage, also commonly known as "optimisation". Here, we take out the dead-weed. We keep and strengthen on the parts of the campaigns which work well, which in turn helps to scale your Google Ads account, cut costs, and improve conversions by allowing for more leads, sales, or whatever your goals and objectives are.

The optimisation you carry out will ultimately determine the profitability and success of your Google Ads account.

Optimising Google Ads campaign is a skill, which takes years to develop. However, in this book, we discuss some basic optimisations you can carry out as a starting point.

Why do we need to optimise?

You can go out and build the best campaign in the world. You can research all year long, conduct thorough keyword research, create awesome Ads, hire the best website developers to build your website landing pages. But ultimately, it is your end users who will determine how and if they engage with your Ads, which keywords they use to come onto your website and so much more. Each time you make changes to your Google Ads, you can bet your bottom dollar, your competitors are doing the same. There are billions of combinations of user-behaviours, which makes it impossible to have a 'perfect' Google Ads account.

You, therefore, need to stay ahead of the game. Understanding what users are typing into search engines to find you, which ads they click on which generate you profit as well as which Ads they click on which drive no conversions.

More so recently it has become more complex with the introduction of Google's machine learning where we now have Smart bidding algorithms, which is where Google does a lot of the guesswork for you, by using the intelligence it has, although not sharing the intelligence with us.

As a result, we use a data-driven approach to optimising. We let the numbers do the talking. Based on the numbers, we make changes to the account to improve its performance, improve profitability, more sales, and that's what optimisation is and why we need it.

How often should you be optimising?

There is no real fixed answer to this, as it really does depend on the size of the account, and what you are spending. For example, an account which is spending $1,000 per month, would require far less work and attention compared to an account that might be spending $100,000 per month.

However, what I would say, is when optimising, ensure you have enough days data to work with. Looking only at the last 24 hours' data for a small account could potentially be misleading, as a drop in conversions for example, could have been caused by external factors, even as simple as the weather, or school holidays. It is therefore fair to say that a reasonable number of days of data would be at least 7 to 14 days, again, it all depends on the size of your Google Ads account.

In the next section, I will go into more detail about the types of optimisations I conduct, but for now, I usually break down my optimisation tasks by week, month & quarterly.

Weekly optimisation tasks

Here I am checking general things such as my keyword, negative keyword, which ads are performing and those that are not, what's costing me a lot of money but not driving any sales, can I see any emerging patterns of something going well, as well as any potential alarm bells that I need to be aware of.

Monthly optimisation tasks

I usually carry this out during the first week of each month. This is where I stand back and look at more of a macro level. What have we really achieved last month? What went well? What did not go so well? I then look at strategies I can develop moving forward, experiments I can perform (for example testing different bidding strategies, or landing pages etc). As a result, I can steer the way forward by looking at a reasonable number of days' data.

Quarterly optimisation tasks

For quarterly optimisation tasks, not only do we look at the Google Ads account but need to understand more about the business itself. We need to check that to ensure what did during the last quarter, was in-line with business objectives. Likewise, moving forward, what strategies do we need to implement to ensure they are in-line with the business objectives. These can be:

- Financial, i.e. Revenue generated, ROI, other Key Performance Indicators (KPIs)
- Products or Services to promote which could be seasonal. i.e., for furniture, maybe the next lot of promotions will be around outdoor furniture for summer.
- Number of new customers acquired as well as setting targets for the next quarter.

We also need to review where are we currently advertising, and what other advertising platforms can we advertise on, this could be anything from:

- Video marketing (.e. YouTube)
- Display
- Retargeting
- … and so on

What optimisation tasks should we be carrying out?

There are so many ways in which you can improve your account by optimising it, in order to run a profitable and successful Google Ads account. I have listed a few different optimisation tasks which we do regularly when optimising Google Ads accounts within our agency. I will not go into each and every option, but more so give you a good guide on the most impactful options for optimising your Google Ads account to help grow your business.

Prioritise Your Optimisation

First and foremost, prioritise your optimisation tasks based on the factors that have the greatest impact on your business, whether that be revenue generated, costs, number of conversions etc.

I am naturally therefore drawn to the campaigns that have the highest spend levels but have low number of conversions or low ROAS (Return on Ad Spend).

Decide internally what your core focus or weekly priorities are going to be for your business.

Campaign Optimisation

Again, my initial focus goes to the higher spending campaigns, and I usually glance at all campaigns to see whether I can see any alarm bells, i.e., a campaign has spent a lot of money but has not resulted in conversions or revenue.

Types of things you can look at a Campaign level are:
- **Bid strategies**.
  - o Is the bid strategy you are using efficient and the most appropriate one. For example, you may have been using Manual CPC. However, is it time to switch to a smart bid strategy such as Maximize Conversion as an example.
  - o Have we set a Target Cost-Per-Action and is the value we set, still the correct one.

o Have we set a Maximum Cost-Per-Click? Maybe our CPCs are too high, so it is always a good idea to have a value.

- **Location**.
  o Are we targeting the correct locations?
  o Have we excluded locations which we do not wish to cater for.
  o Have we set the right 'Detailed location options' to ensure we are only targeting people who are within the areas we are targeting.

- **Device**.
  o Hopefully, it may not surprise you to know over 60% of traffic to most sites comes from mobile phones. Looking at your Device settings you can see a breakdown of conversions for Mobile Computer and Tablet. So, here's the question... Which device is costing you a lot of money in terms of clicks, but not generating you any conversions? These would be the devices that you can Bid Down on which is a way of telling Google to spend less on these devices. Similarly, you can choose to Bid Up on the profitable devices.

- **Ad Schedule**.
  o This is one that is usually under-estimated. Think about what day of the week your customers usually buy. Similarly, what time of the day are they more likely to buy. You

can use the Google Ads Reports to get this information which we will cover in the next section. Then you simply adjust the Ad Schedule to tell Google, which days of the week you would like your Ads to appear as well as what time of the day. What's the point in paying for clicks on certain days or hours of the day which are not profitable?

Ad Group Optimisation

Click into a campaign. Which campaign? You decide. You create your list of priorities in terms of which campaign you wish to click on first so that you can review the Ad groups within it.

As a first point of call, I always base my priority based on those that are spending a lot of money, but either:

- Lack conversions
- Conversion Rate is low
- Cost Per Action is high

I do this as these are clearly the campaigns that require the most amount of attention.

There are so many factors that can influence why an Ad group might be performing poorly, which include Keywords and Ads, which we will cover in the next section.
So, from an Ad group perspective, more importantly, I check to see if there are missed opportunities. I ask questions such as:

- Have I covered all themes which are relevant to the campaign? In other words, are there other groups I need to add?
- Are there Ad groups which may be too similar, so may actually benefit from being consolidated into one Ad group, for ease of maintenance?
- Which Ad group do I need to click into first to examine it more closely?
- Review to see if all Keywords within an Ad group are correctly themed and are relevant to one another.

Keyword Optimisation

I usually find that this is where I end up spending most of my time. Analysing Keywords. There is so much you can do here, but some of the most basics include:

- **Quality Score**
  - Look at your Quality Score for keywords. I usually first apply a filter to show me keywords which have received more than "x" number of clicks. In this way, I know I'm only looking at keywords which have been costly or are in demand. I can then focus my time and attention on these. I then sort by lowest quality score. This is where the fun really starts, to see why the quality score,

maybe so low. There could be numerous reasons from:

- Low budget
- Low Click-Through-Rate (CTR). See what you can to help increase your CTR. Maybe amend your Ad copy in your Headlines and ensure your Ad Strength is good.
- The Keywords may not be highly relevant to the Ad group and Ads. This could be a sign that your Ad groups are not organised well too.

- **Search Terms**
  - ○ Remember, **keywords** are what you have told Google you want your Ads shown on the Google pages for, but **Search Terms** is what the user actually used to find your Ads. Although you have specified Keywords, depending on the match type, and other factors such as close variations of the keywords, synonyms etc, you can see this information by clicking on the 'Search terms' tab. Checking your search terms should therefore be done as often as possible, depending on the size of your account.

    So, what do you do by looking at search terms?

Look for search terms which have keywords in them, that are not relevant to your business. In which case you can Add these as "Negative Keywords" For example, see the following table:

Keyword	Match Types	Possible Search Terms
"office chairs"	Phrase	• Leather office chairs • Office chair designer • Office chair repairs • Cost of office chairs

Looking at the table above, we can see some search terms which were triggered by this keyword which may not be relevant, i.e., "**designer**" – As this is possibly someone who is looking for a designer, as well as "**repairs**" – Maybe this is a service you do not provide. In this case, you can add "designer" and "repairs" as a **Negative keyword**, which means moving forward, your ad will not show for search terms which contain these words:

- **Match Types**
  - o We discussed what match types are in setting up Ad the groups section. Depending on how you use your Match Types, it will have a huge impact on your account's performance. It is therefore absolutely imperative you understand how to optimise match

types. So, what optimisation can we do for match types? As always there are numerous ways to do any task in Google. I have therefore listed two of the most common ways I use to optimise Match Types.

- Separating
  - So that you can better analyse performance of match types, it sometimes helps to separate them into their own Ad Groups. For example, you might wish to put Exact Match keywords into one ad group and Phrase into another. In this case, it is important that you ensure you have the negative keyword equivalent in the Phrase Match, i.e., ensure that for the keywords you have in the Phrase Match, you have added their Exact Match equivalent as negative keywords. Furthermore, if you separate keywords into Campaigns, you have better control over budgets too, i.e., you may wish to only spend a small percentage of your budget on Broad Match compared to Exact Match.
- Costs and Conversions / you're your KPIs
  - Analyse which match types may be costing you a lot of money but not driving you any conversions! In which case, you need to decide whether you keep those match types, or do you minimise your spend on them.

Device Optimisation

What device are your ads being shown on? When I talk about devices, I'm referring to Mobile, Desktop Computer or Tablets. When it comes to optimisation, you need to look at the statistics to see which devices are your conversions coming from? In which case, Google Ads allows you to adjust your bids, so that you bid more on these. Likewise, which device may be costing you a lot of money but are not generating you any conversions. In this case, you need to do something called a negative bid adjustment. For example, if you find that on Tablets, you are wasting your money, you can say to Google, bid down on this device by 20%, or whatever you wish.

Location Optimisation

Think about the areas you wish to target. It's good to be a big fish in a small pond rather than a small fish in a big pond. This means that you will have better control of your budget too as it is being more focused to the area that you wish to serve.

To help with this you can also look at the report available by taking on the report's option at the top of the Google page and looking at the predefined location reports. Such reports will show you where most of your clicks are coming from but more importantly where your conversions may be coming from. You can then decide to adjust your location settings so that they are showing ads to people in areas which are driving you more conversions.

Day / Hour Optimisation

Depending on which industry you are in or which products or services you sell, potential buyers will be looking at your ads or inquiring about your products or services during different days of the week as well as different times of the day.

An example of this is if you have a furniture website. you may find that during the daytime your potential buyers are at work and are therefore not able to make a purchase. this could simply be because they may wish to consult their partner first in which case, they are more likely to buy or inquire during the evenings.

In both cases above, you have the ability to optimise your ad scheduling so that you add only appear during certain days of the week as well as certain hours of the day. Similarly, it is possible to adjust your ad scheduling so that your ads do not appear at all during certain days of the week. For example, you may be closed on a Sunday and may not be able to take telephone calls. In this case, it makes sense to adjust your ad scheduling so that your ads do not appear on Sundays which means that you are saving money and avoiding wasted clicks.

On a final note, if we were to get more advanced, we might like to take into account that certain people may research on a specific date of the week but make the actual purchase on another day of the week. For example, people may wish to research on a Sunday but make a purchase on a Monday. My point being when adjusting your ad scheduling it's important that you test, test and test to see what the impact of your bid adjustments may have resulted in.

Bid Strategy Optimisation

In the <u>Budget and Bidding</u> section, we discussed the various bidding strategies that are available within Google ads. A common mistake is people set a bidding strategy and forget to review it. It is absolutely imperative that you keep on top of your big strategy to ensure it is the correct one. For example, when you first launch a campaign, you may have decided to use the Manual CPC strategy. It is now time to take a look to see how many conversions you have and how old how many clicks you had on your website. Ideally, in order to switch to a smart bidding strategy such as maximise conversions you need at least 15 conversions within the last 30 days. This is a bit of a debatable subject as many people including Google themselves now suggest that it is possible to use a smart bidding strategy even if you have fewer conversions in the last 30 days as the algorithm is clever enough to work out the biding it needs to use for your keywords.

The great news is Google ads allow you to conduct something called "**Experiments**". Experiments can be used where you may wish you try a bid strategy but may not wish to fully commit to it yet as you do not know how it will perform. In this case, you can set up an experiment telling Google that although you are currently using a specific bid strategy for example manual CPC, you wish to try a different bid strategy such as maximise conversions. Furthermore, you can specify a percentage, in other words, you can say to Google that you wish to keep 60% of your traffic towards the current bid strategy i.e. manual CPC, but only 40% towards the new strategy which you wish to test i.e. maximise conversions. after running the experiment for a few days, I would suggest at least two weeks, you will easily and quickly be able to see how each bid strategy performed and can then make a decision as to whether you already to now change to the new bid strategy or you wish to keep the existing one that you have.

Budget Optimisation

In addition to optimising various factors by reading your Google ads account, you may also wish to review your budget in terms of firstly, are we on track with our weekly or monthly spend? The common problem that I see in many accounts whereby budgets run over as they have not been reviewed in a timely fashion. So, depending on the size of your account you need to decide how often you need to review your budget to make sure that you are not overspending and at the same time make sure that you are not significantly under spending too.

I also suggest taking a look at campaigns which may be delivering great results but may be limited by budget. In which case increase in the budget within these campaigns could lead to more conversions as a quick win. Please remember that when increasing budgets, I suggest only increasing in the region of around 10% to 15% at a time and letting the campaign run for at least seven days before making another adjustment. Making huge adjustments in one go, may need your account to go back into **learning mode** again. Campaigns go into Learning Mode when Google has to learn again, how best to bid on your keywords. This is normally triggered by what Google may consider, a reasonable number of changes within a short period of time.

Following on from the above in a similar fashion if you find you have campaigns which are underperforming, and you have conducted all the other optimizations it may be time to reduce the budget under your campaigns.

Impression Share

Impression share is a great way to see what percentage of the time your Ads are actually showing up on Google. Googles definition is:

What is impression share in Google ads?

> "Impression share (IS) is the percentage of impressions that your ads receive compared to the total number of impressions that your ads could get. Impression share = impressions / total eligible impressions."

There are various factors that can influence your Impression share, some of which include

- Budget
- Max CPC
- Quality of your Ads

- Targeting settings

You need to go through these and look at any other factor that may be influencing your impression share if you feel your impression share is low.

Review "Recommendations"

On the second navigation panel which is on the left-hand side OK Google ads. The screen you will see an option called recommendations. It is worth clicking on this option periodically as Google will make recommendations as to how you can improve the performance of your Google ads account. A word of caution is not to believe everything Google suggests. I usually only agree with a roundabout 40% of Google's recommendations. And that's because I understand my websites and my clients' websites a lot better than Google's algorithm. So, for me, it's not only about looking at the numbers but the quality of various factors such as the keywords and so on. So, if you have been given a recommendation which you do not agree with simply click on it and click on dismiss. As a result of this, you will now be left with recommendations that you are happy to look further into and apply to your campaigns if appropriate.

18) Step 7 - Audit

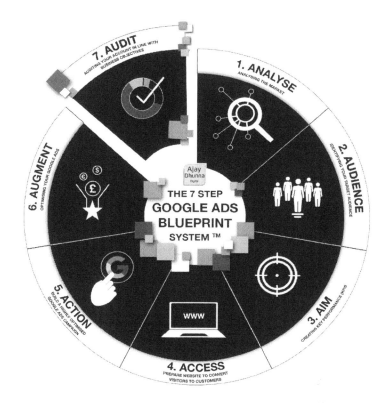

By conducting a regular audit on your Google ads account, not only would you find areas of improvement, but also areas where you can save money and get more conversions. You would also use this to discover new opportunities which you may not have yet been aware of or considered. Furthermore, by auditing your account periodically you also need to make sure that you are in line with your monthly quarterly or yearly objectives.

Contrary to popular myths, Google Ads is not a Plug and Play system. Automation does not mean you set something up and it will run forever itself. Remember, Google always wins. Regardless of whether you get enquiries / sales or not, they are taking your hard-earned money. So please avoid putting 100% trust into their algorithm, as they will love you for it!

Google ads is one of the most comprehensive and complicated digital marketing platforms available to date. It is therefore important that audits are conducted on a regular basis. We do this by following a structure, to help ensure we have not missed anything out.

As an agency, each time we take on a brand-new client who may already have an existing campaign, we always conduct an audit first. By doing so, it helps us to create a roadmap of everything that needs to be done, as well as highlighting areas that require urgent attention.

So now let's get into the areas I look at when conducting audits.

Website

As obvious as this sounds the very first thing, I always check is the website. And this is because the website is ultimately usually where we send help potential visitors to when they click on our Ads. Many of the items I check for have been covered in the Access section of this book. But essentially, it's things like:

- Is the website even working?

- Is the navigation working?
- Speed of website.
- Do they even have unique landing pages for the products or services wish to promote? Ideally you should have unique landing pages for each of your campaigns.
- Good call directions.

Conversion Tracking

"What gets measured gets done"…
- [Peter Drucker]

Unsurprisingly this is where I find most of the initial problems within the Google ads audit.

Google Analytics

Firstly, ensure that the Google ads account has been correctly linked and set up with Google Analytics. Although we have not covered Google Analytics in great detail, it is the main tool that will give you in-depth data as to the behaviours of your website visitors.

Goals

Goals is what you would use in order to track your conversions. Conversions can be anything from telephone calls, someone filling in a form on your website, someone making a purchase on your website, someone subscribing to a newsletter on your website, emailing you from your website and so on. It is up to you to define which conversions you wish to track. My recommendation is to focus on conversions which are tangible to your business, for example, if someone fills in an inquiry form that's a potentially tangible benefit to your business. If, however somebody visits your page, I would not classify that as a tangible benefit. I say this because I'm always shocked at the amount of conversion tracking, I see where people are classifying an important part of your website or a page on the website classified as a conversion.

By having goals and conversions set up, not only is it helping you to understand which of your campaigns, Ad groups, keywords etc are working, but more importantly, this data let Google's smart bidding algorithms use to determine how they should bid on various keywords.

*"The quality of your conversion tracking is paramount. I commonly used the phrase **GIGO**, which stands for "Garbage In Garbage Out"; if you feed Google with garbage information, i.e., poor tracking, it's going to give you garbage results, i.e. costly and less profitable campaigns."*

Structure of your Campaigns and Ad Groups

Review the structure of your campaigns and add groups and assess whether they are in line with your business objectives your products and your services. You also need to assess the campaigns that are doing very well compared to those that may require more attention. When looking at your campaign settings it is also important to drill down into each aspect of that campaign. For example:

- bid strategies
- location settings
- ad scheduling
- device targeting

Ads and Extensions

Your ads are ultimately what your potential customers will read and as a result determine whether they wish to click on them or click on your competitors' ads. Check each ad group to ensure you have at least two to three ads. Furthermore, check to ensure that the ads that you do have are driving your conversions. At this point in time, it is also a good idea to ensure the ad copy is good and well written. Not only do you wish to attract people to click on the ads, but you also wish to disqualify people from clicking on your ads if your products or services are not suitable for them. Always keep in account **click-through-rate** (**CTR**) is one of the most important metrics Google users to determine your quality score.

Next, we need to ensure that you are using the main extensions for each of your campaigns and ad groups which we covered in an earlier section. Buy extensions I mean things like:

- Sitelinks
- Call extensions
- Callout extensions
- Image extensions
- Location extensions
- Etc.

Search Terms

Go through the search terms to ensure that they are all relevant to your products and services. For those that are not add them as negative keywords. Use this as an opportunity to discover new keywords too. If you do discover new keywords that you have not thought of, add them as keywords with the appropriate match type with the appropriate ad group.

Reporting

To help with all the above, Google has a reporting section which contains some predefined reports.

You can access the predefined reports by clicking on
- Reports
- Predefined reports (Dimensions)
- Then selecting which report you want to see.

It would not be possible for me to talk through every single report because there are too many of these. However, I suggest going through each of these and picking out the report that you wish to take a look at on a regular basis.

What's great is that you can firstly customise then Save these reports, and can also download the reports onto your computer, or schedule these reports to the emailed over to you periodically e.g., monthly.

19) Some Final Thoughts

I have pretty much said what I wanted to say in this book. I seriously can go on and on. It's been difficult for me to write this book... very difficult. As I'm more of a practical person, so reading and writing is not really in my forte. However, I'm truly passionate about what I do, and want to help as many people and businesses as possible. With that in mind, I have a few additional quick nuggets of thoughts and suggestions for those who may wish to embark on the journey of implementing Google Ads strategies for their business.

Google Analytics

This has to be an absolute Must for every business. If you do not have it installed or are not sure, get in touch with a marketeer and ask them to check.

Managing customer expectations

Don't sell your customers a dream. Your customer will want results tomorrow. Even for brand new campaigns. It is your job to manage their expectations. During my two-decades or so of managing customers, I've learnt, it is best to educate your customers, set realistic expectations, instead of trying to simply win their business by telling them what they wish to hear. Such strategies are short-lived, and you will end up working every hour of the day, to retain that customer!

Recruiting the right staff

For me, in my digital marketing agency, it has always been to hire people, who have a passion for what they are applying for, whether it be Google Ads, or building websites. I'm a firm believer of productivity over the "9 till 5" mentality. The financial rewards are just a bi-product of the hard work, and the passion you put into the work you do.

You don't have to hire the best of the best. If you already have great staff who are willing to train, hire those who are willing to learn and haven't spent the last two-decades working for people such as "that yellow directory" company, who prey on short-cuts to monetising from their clients from building sub-standard campaigns which attract their customers!

Outsource of DIY? (Do It Yourself)?

There is no real answer. If you outsource, are you equipped with some knowledge about what to look out for when hiring a freelancer or agency. I'm hoping that by reading this book, you will be well on your way. As you will stand a much better chance of getting better results from your marketing agency or freelancer, simply because they know, you are asking the right questions and are not starting off on a blank sheet!

If you do however decide you take the DIY approach, that's also good. As long as you continually update your knowledge, what's working, what isn't working so well with Google Ads, strategies, new features and so much more.

In my personal opinion, do what you know best. Focus on building and serving your customers. Leave the rest to the experts who do this day-in, day-out!

Here at my agency, we have a full team. A team that specialises in understanding customer requirements to build the campaign right from day one. We have a team who specialises in optimising Google Ads campaigns day-in-day out. They even have Optimisation & Eggs for breakfast! We have expert copy-writers and so much more. If you feel you are adequately equipped with handling the day to day running of your Google Ads account as well as troubleshooting, then be my guest. Else, reach out and let's have a chat about how we can help your business grow!

20) What Next?

First and foremost, I Thank you unconditionally for taking the time to buy this book and to go through it.

Implement things you have learned, or ask your team members, your agency, questions based on your learning.

It has taken me years of hard work, losing lots of money, and working on hundreds of Google Ads accounts to really understand what makes Google Ads works.

I'm here to help you fast-track your success and avoid the costly mistakes I have made. If you have any questions about anything written inside the book, or want help with your Google Ads / digital marketing, please feel free to reach out to me using my contact details below, or emailing me personally on ajay@ajaydhunna.com.

Similarly, maybe you are just starting out on your journey to business, and may wish to discuss the Do's and Don'ts when it comes to marketing. Whatever the case, feel free to reach out to me as we also have various digital marketing mentoring and training programs

As promised...

You qualify for a Free Google Ads Audit!

Not only will the review look at your Google Ads, we will look at other factors which may help your business to grow, such as your website, how well your website is performing on organic Google (SEO) and so much more. You will get a video personally recorded by myself.

Book your Free Google Ads Audit by visiting www.ajaydhunna.com/freereview

Remember to mention in the description, "Claiming My Free PPC Audit as per your book"

I would also like you to join me on my YouTube channel where I publish weekly videos as well as my Instagram

For this go to:

YouTube:		https://youtube.com/ajaydhunna

Instagram:		https://instagram.com/ajaydhunnaofficial

If you wish to reach out to be, visit my website and feel free to get in touch on www.ajaydhunna.com

You could also visit this link: https://qrco.de/ajaydhunna or scan this QR code for all these links:

Printed in Great Britain
by Amazon

87277111R00138